VGM Opportunities Series

OPPORTUNITIES IN **INTERIOR DESIGN AND DECORATING CAREERS**

Victoria Kloss Ball

Revised by
David Stearns, ASID

Foreword by
Charles D. Gandy, FASID, IIDA

VGM Career Horizons
a division of *NTC Publishing Group*
Lincolnwood, Illinois USA

Cover Photo Credits:

Lower right photograph courtesy of David Stearns, ASID. All other photographs courtesy of Kendall College of Art & Design.

Library of Congress Cataloging-in-Publication Data

Ball, Victoria Kloss.
Opportunities in interior design and decorating careers / Victoria Kloss Ball ; revised by David Stearns ; foreword by Charles D. Gandy.
p. cm.
Includes bibliographical references.
ISBN 0-8442-4440-6 (hard). — ISBN 0-8442-4441-4 (soft)
1. Interior decoration—Vocational guidance—United States.
I. Stearns, David. II. Title.
NK2116.B3 1995
729′.023′73—dc20 94-47112
CIP

Published by VGM Career Horizons, a division of NTC Publishing Group
4255 West Touhy Avenue
Lincolnwood (Chicago), Illinois 60646-1975, U.S.A.

Manufactured in the United States of America.

5 6 7 8 9 0 VP 9 8 7 6 5 4 3 2 1

CONTENTS

About the Authors . . . . **vi**

Acknowledgments . . . . **ix**

Foreword . . . . **xi**

1. Understanding Interior Design **1**

What is interior design? Disciplines within interior design. A science or an art? Science: what is it? Art: what is it and who is the artist?

2. The Profession of Interior Design **11**

A business and a profession. Beginning a project. Programming. Duration of design relations. Types of interiors with respect to functions. Methods of receiving payment. Types of interior design firms. The interior designer's supplies. The designer's need for skilled craftworkers. The human factor. Working conditions. Remuneration.

3. Your School and You 41

Student organizations. Educational costs. Financial aid. Selecting a school. A word of advice.

4. Educational and Personal Requirements . . . 53

High school preparation. The state of education. Formal education: its content. Kinds of programs. Your qualifications. Business potential.

5. Getting Started—Employment 71

Where to apply. Experience requirement. Applying for positions. The resume. The interview. After the interview. Professionalism. Advancement. Leaving a position. Employment prospects.

6. Custom Designing 87

A studio of your own. The start. Importance of custom design.

7. Contract Designing 93

The client and the firm. The suppliers. The financial aspect of contract designing. Advantages and disadvantages for the young designer. How the work progresses. You and the contract firm. Contract design and the future.

8. Related Fields **103**

Opportunities within the professional career. Opportunities for those with professional or paraprofessional training.

9. Professional Organizations **117**

Defining a profession. Why professional organizations exist. The American Institute of Interior Design (AIID). The American Society of Interior Designers (ASID). Interior Design Educators Council (IDEC). Foundation of Interior Design Education Research (FIDER). International Federation of Interior Designers (IFI). Industry Foundation of ASID. National Council for Interior Design Qualification (NCIDQ). Interior Designers of Canada (IDC). Licensing.

10. International Interior Design **129**

Similarities and differences. Professional organization. American interior design ideas abroad. Formal education exchange.

11. The Future of Interior Design **135**

A bright future. Large enterprises. Standardization of products. New science and technology. A different market. The challenge.

A Final Word **143**

ABOUT THE AUTHORS

Victoria Kloss Ball is professor emeritus of interior design at Case Western Reserve University, Cleveland, Ohio. After receiving her Ph.D. in art from that institution in 1942, she was in charge of the program of interior design, teaching in the departments of art, architecture, and home economics. She has been a member of a number of professional societies, including the College Art Association of America, the American Institute of Interior Designers (honorary member), the Interior Design Educators Council (fellow), the Furniture History Society, the National Trust for Historic Preservation, the American Society of Architectural Historians, the American Society for Aesthetics, and the Inter-society Color Council. She is author of the two-volume *The History of Architecture and Interior Design* (Wiley) and *The Art of Interior Design* (Macmillan, 1960; rev. Wiley, 1980), and she has written several encyclopedia articles on the educational aspects of interior design.

David Stearns received his graduate degree in interior design at Case Western Reserve University, Cleveland,

Ohio, in 1964. He has taught interior design at Auburn University, Auburn, Alabama, and was author of the first professional interior design curriculum at the University of Tennessee, Knoxville. He has taught interior design at the University of British Columbia, Vancouver; the University of Memphis; and the University of Mississippi.

He was secretary to the Interior Design Educators Council (IDEC) and is a professional member of the American Society of Interior Designers (ASID). He has served the Tennessee chapter as president and member to the national board of directors, ASID.

He has practiced interior design for the past 24 years and is licensed by the state of Tennessee as an interior designer.

ACKNOWLEDGMENTS

This book is of necessity indebted to the entire interior design profession for its material. We hope that all aspects of the profession have been given adequate, accurate, and appropriate coverage. It must be made clear, however, that the author accepts responsibility for all statements made herein.

FOREWORD

Interior design. It is a world where creativity breeds innovation and today's trends become tomorrow's styles. It is a career that links complex problems with unique solutions. It is a field in which art mingles freely with science to transform an architectural shell into a total environment.

Interior design is a profession that is as demanding as it is rewarding. No longer is today's design professional simply someone with artistic flair or good taste. The successful designer must also employ a wide range of skills: problem definition, program analysis, and space planning. Likewise, he or she must possess specific technical knowledge of construction, codes, zoning laws, fire regulations, product technology, and product sources in order to create functional as well as aesthetically pleasing interiors.

In the nearly twenty-five years I've been a practicing designer, I've witnessed changes in an industry which has grown dramatically in size as well as in its level of professionalism. Demographic changes, such as the two-career couple, an aging population, and the single parent household, have led more and more consumers to seek the assistance of designers in matching their lifestyles with their residences. With the link between interior design and office productivity becoming increasingly evident and with the growing acceptance of the home office, corporate America is also turning to the professional designer to provide the services which will affect their bottom line.

Career opportunities in this growing field are limitless. In addition to designing residential and office interiors, you may specialize in such commercial spaces as hotels, restaurants, schools, hospitals, stores, and government buildings—just to name a few. You can even choose to specialize in one aspect of interior design such as space planning, color consultation, or teaching. Throughout my career, I'm proud to have taken advantage of the diversity inherent in this field by applying my skills not only toward interior design but toward product design and design education.

But with opportunity inevitably comes responsibility—the responsibility to prepare yourself as best as you can to accept the challenges of an increasingly competitive marketplace. A solid educational background can provide you with specialized knowledge in such growth areas as energy-efficient design, interiors for disabled people, adaptive use of buildings, and environmental safety.

Throughout the following pages, you will discover the many roles which you, as a future designer, must adopt—artist and entrepreneur, innovator and businessperson, listener and communicator, employer and client—the roles which allow you to be the best you can be in shaping the environments we all share.

Good reading and welcome to a most exciting and stimulating career!

Charles D. Gandy, FASID, IIDA
President, Gandy/Peace, Inc., Atlanta, Georgia
National President, American Society of Interior Designers (1988)
ASID Designer of Distinction (1994)

CHAPTER 1

UNDERSTANDING INTERIOR DESIGN

WHAT IS INTERIOR DESIGN?

Interior designers plan and provide for the insides of buildings in order to make them as functional, beautiful, and meaningful as possible. They direct the work that is necessary to achieve this result.

It sometimes is difficult to separate the career of interior design from other careers dealing with similar problems. This possible overlapping often creates a certain confusion in academic organization as well as in practice. Training for interior design may be found under various established departments such as art, architecture, human ecology, and home economics in an academic curriculum.

Following is a list of some career disciplines related to interior design that are in present catalogues.

Disciplines Concerned with the Environment

- Environmental planning
- Space planning: regional and city

- Construction engineering
- Architecture
- Landscape architecture
- Interior design
- Ecology: the interrelation between humans and their environment
- Design as related to the home

DISCIPLINES WITHIN INTERIOR DESIGN

There are numerous disciplines within the career of interior design. These wide-ranging disciplines include the following:

Disciplines Concerned with Structure

- Of materials, such as woods, fabrics, glass, synthetics, plastics, ceramics, stones, metals, colorants, finishes
- Of elaborate artifacts, such as furniture, cabinets, walls, windows, doors
- Of building equipment systems

Disciplines Concerned with Function

- Performance of materials
- Performance of equipment
- Interior space utilization

Disciplines Concerned with Specialized Performance

- Toxicity
- Fire prevention
- Safety
- Air conditioning
- Illumination

Disciplines Concerned with Special Group Needs

- Age groups
- The handicapped
- The sick

Disciplines Needed for Business

- Business principles and procedures
- Organizing and managing an interior design business
- Knowledge of details of an interior design business: sources, estimates, specifications, ordering, receiving, installing, billing, cost-accounting

Computer Technology

- For presentations
- For data recall
- For business management

Presentation Skills

- Presentation techniques: drafting, rendering, model making, photography, designing with computers, speaking

Craft Skills

- Knowledge of crafts such as weaving, carpentry

Social Disciplines

- Working with, for, and through the agency of other people

Promotional Disciplines

- Writing and speaking
- Organizational work

Professional Disciplines

- Knowledge of and working under a professional code
- Working with others in the same profession

Aesthetic Disciplines

- Designing of interior details
- Interior space planning from the visual point of view
- Color and light planning in relation to space
- Color and light, art and science interrelations—used for effective lighting and paint technology
- Texture planning

Academic Disciplines with Cultural Implications

- Economics
- History
- Language
- Literature
- Mathematics
- Psychology
- Physical sciences
- Sociology

A SCIENCE OR AN ART?

The preceding lists show that interior design encompasses an understanding of many disciplines. This raises a question: Is interior design a science or an art? It is both, of course. In the twentieth century there are few subjects that do not involve scientific material. Interior design not only includes some matter of pure science, such as is found in the study of color and illumination, but also makes use of a vast amount of information that could be classified as applied science or technology, such as computer drafting.

Interior design is likewise an art—one of the most complex and perhaps one of the most important. Did you ever stop to think how much space it occupies in our art museums?

Because of this dual nature, interior design is a challenging subject that appeals to people who enjoy life in both scientific and aesthetic terms.

SCIENCE: WHAT IS IT?

In science (using the term, as we shall, to include both pure and applied examples), the method employed to gain a result is a matter of precise knowledge. Therefore, the facts of science can be taught and its dictates must be followed to solve many objective problems.

For instance, an architect must master such knowledge as the manner of constructing a building so that it will stand, bear its load, enclose a satisfactory climate, and provide adequate illumination. Such structural knowledge likewise relates to the interior of a building. The interior designer must know which are the loadbearing walls since they must not be destroyed unless there are reinforcements to compensate. How much weight can a partition support? What is the relation between any change in the design of a fireplace and its performance?

Because equipment is now fairly standardized and can be described in objective terms, the functioning of performing areas is nearly an exact science. The current trend is toward even greater standardization, and this fact alone makes interior design a growing technological subject. It is only because of these objective data that specification writing for a job has become so possible and necessary.

This objectivity has extended into space planning, making it something of a technological subject. We know the space required by a person walking or for groups engaged in conversation. We know the standardized sizes of kitchen and bath equipment, storage space, and comfortable space for dining.

More than that, scientists tell us that we can measure some of the psychological aspects of space; for example, how much is required for psychological ease, at what point claustrophobia begins to set in, and when space is so vast that it loses its "human" quality. If you think these are foolish considerations, try renting a series of apartments of varying sizes and listen to the comments.

Try to project some of this objective knowledge about space into phases of interior design that are still in their infancy. Is there any change in space demands for the elderly, for the sick, for the child at school?

There are some disciplines that lie in the border territory between art and science. Market disciplines are such. For example, the designer must understand the price market and the economic theories that govern it.

The computer discipline certainly comes under the scientific heading of technology. It is not always an easy one to master.

And so it goes. There is so much that a qualified interior designer should know that falls under the heading of science, or exact knowledge, that sometimes one wonders whether it has been forgotten that the subject of interior design is more importantly an art.

ART: WHAT IS IT AND WHO IS THE ARTIST?

Now we enter a discussion that should be foremost in every school that has an interior design curriculum. There is a tendency to forget that interior design is an art, and it can be an important art. It is more than a core of disciplines that can be routinely taught and easily learned. Good art is not of that nature.

First, the materials and organization of art are basic to life. Art is manipulation of the ingredients of life—usually sensuous material because the senses are avenues for the entrance of life—to move people emotionally and often intellectually, to help them see life with new eyes. Their sensations and their thoughts are changed in the process. Art is the organization of details in order to achieve such aesthetic stimulation.

Second, the response to art is individual. People view art with their own eyes, never with yours. They can profess to like what they are told is good art; they may even copy its most identifiable characteristics. However, they often have the notes but not the music. They must make the acquaintance of great art continually if they are to create it. Great art can change people because it changes the perceptions.

Third, people can grow in an appreciation of art. Good art is always what we choose to call beautiful. When you have created it, it is not certain that everyone will immediately recognize it. But beauty in and of itself creates sensitivity. It creates an avenue for growing appreciation.

Beauty in interior design carries the idea of an emotional pleasure that joins the mind and the senses in a form which is directly related to use. This brings up the question of taste, because what may seem to be the right solution to one person may not appeal to another. Taste, as the word is used here, often carries the idea of a personal preference that is not only strong but also bears the suggestion of being akin to the taste of the discerning.

As such it should not be ridiculed. However, it is liable to be baffled by dissenting voices and a client who has his or her own decided opinions. This interaction between art, designer, and patron is a difficult consideration for all the environment arts. When dealing with an environment that lies close to people, it is not good for a person to assume that he or she knows the only answer.

A workable professional interior design solution must include that reciprocity between client and designer that produces an answer understandable and pleasing to both parties. This is not necessarily in the nature of a compromise which may please neither; it is a treaty which will give each satisfaction.

This discussion about the science and art of interior design can emphasize only one conclusion. Because interior design is both a difficult and worthwhile endeavor, it is hoped that you will enter it with the determination to go to a good school in order to appreciate the entire scope of what you should learn. For although it is sometimes necessary and quite possible to go where you will have adequate training in one phase or another of interior design, it is quite a different thing to learn the lessons of good art and good science and the fusing of them through good design.

CHAPTER 2

THE PROFESSION OF INTERIOR DESIGN

A BUSINESS AND A PROFESSION

Interior design may be defined as both a business and a profession. The two terms need not be exclusive.

It has often been somewhat facetiously said that a job is work for pay while a career is trained work engaged in for an appreciable period of time for compensation; similarly, business is the buying and selling for the best possible monetary profit while a profession provides a worthwhile service requiring much knowledge at a reward fixed by ethical considerations. We shall not quarrel with the last two definitions, although we can claim that the "bottom line" need not be the only consideration in business nor the altruistic motive necessarily the only controlling factor in a profession. One's sense of values can enable the two to join in partnership.

One reason for not being too ironbound about the matter of designation is the fact that careers and classifications can change. For example, it has been only a little over two hundred years that the medical profession has been fully acknowledged as a profession.

The first essential qualification for a career to be a profession is that its participating members should as a group bind themselves to educational standards and to an ethical way of conducting their business.

First let us set down the introductory definition of the professional interior designer as endorsed by its largest professional organization, the American Society of Interior Designers (ASID):

> A professional interior designer is a person qualified by education, experience, and examination, who:
>
> 1. identifies, researches, and creatively solves problems pertaining to the function and quality of the interior environment;
> 2. performs services relative to the interior spaces, including programming, design analysis, space planning and aesthetics, using specialized knowledge of interior construction, building codes, equipment, materials, and furnishings;
> 3. prepares drawings and documents relative to the design of interior spaces in order to enhance and protect the health, safety, and welfare of the public.

Further, as outlined in the ASID code of ethics:

> The designer shall at all times consider the health, safety, and welfare of the public in spaces that he or she designs.

> The designer will, before entering into a contract, verbal or written, clearly determine the scope and nature of the project and the method or methods of compensation.
>
> The designer may offer professional services to the client as a consultant, specificer, and/or supplier on the basis of a fee, percentage, or mark-up.
>
> The designer shall have the responsibility of fully disclosing to the client the manner in which all compensation is to be paid.
>
> The designer shall perform services for the client in a manner consistent with the client's best interests, wishes, and preferences, so long as those interests, wishes, and preferences do not violate laws, regulations, and codes, the designer's aesthetic judgment, or the health, safety, or welfare of the occupants.

Because a large majority of interior design is in the contract field where the standardization of products makes the subletting of work possible, interior designers may send some of the specified work out to bids. However, in most instances, this manner of subletting is not feasible even in contract work because the client wishes the designer to keep very close supervision over the project.

Two additional factors prevent interior design from being considered solely a large-quantity piece of production. First, interior design is designing an indoor environment for people. Many times a standardized solution will not answer. Second, how could one write specifications for Van Gogh's *Sunflowers* or an eighteenth-century Kerman oriental carpet? What subcontractor could handle the order? Artistic creativity does not necessarily fit into neat patterns.

A professional person does not buy and sell commodities in a way inconsistent with the agreed-upon ethical stipulations of its professional group. But not all professional groups can adopt the same rules and regulations relative to their operation because not all activities, even within the same profession, are equivalent. For instance, a doctor who delivers a baby may have an hourly fee while a family physician may charge a fixed amount per examination, and a dentist may go up and down the price ladder according to the cost of materials.

The important stipulation is that the parties participating know and agree to the manner of remuneration and that the work be honestly carried out according to the agreement.

Interior design as now professionally practiced can be regarded either as a business conducted in a professional manner or as a profession conducted in an ethical business manner.

BEGINNING A PROJECT

Interior design has changed a great deal over the past quarter of a century. Like our civilization, it operates on a much larger scale than it has in the past, and it is concerned with a broader spectrum of activities; hence, its organizational units are frequently much larger. Some interior design companies are very large indeed.

Nevertheless, it is true that the small company, perhaps having no more than five designers on its staff and often being a one-person concern, has by no means passed out of the picture. This is good. In the small company—in the individual practice—opportunity is given for and advantage can be taken of more personalized relations. We begin here with the small enterprise as our model and in later chapters indicate how other situations differ from this.

What does an interior designer do on a job? Let us consider the situation with a newly trained person who has just entered a small firm.

Just a few years ago such a beginning was regarded as an apprenticeship and was considered good to obtain. It is still a desirable way to begin the career of interior design. However, it is not an apprenticeship in the traditional sense of the word, for the kind of education schools now provide eliminates the need for this type of training. The bygone apprenticeship, with its philosophy of learning in place of salary, has fortunately passed. The neophyte is entitled to a living wage because he or she is expected and is equipped to serve the company adequately for such. In return the apprentice receives the opportunity to work in a real situation and to collect experience.

The first few months on any career—what may be called the novice period—should provide the opportunity to observe all the facets of an operating concern. Among these, of course, is the opportunity to do some designing. Don't hasten this phase of the work until you are certain that you have the details of procedure firmly in your grasp.

We will assume that the particular firm that employs you is most interested in serving the individual private client. (The customer is usually known as a client in the designing field.) Many small firms or individuals going into private practice are not geared to designing for large contracts; their customers are individuals rather than corporations.

Your first engagement in private practice usually involves a talk with your client. How do you get a client? Your superiors may have decided it was time for you to try your wings, so they assign you to one of their less-complicated jobs. Perhaps you have done some work that has been seen and your services may be requested, or maybe your client has met and liked you—after all, liking (among other things) occurs under conditions of similarity of tastes and values.

Your client may have confidence in you as a person. This confidence factor is important in all client decisions, and it is probably a valid reason for choosing one designer over another. And it is certainly built right into the success of a piece of work: if there is no confidence between designer and client, by definition there will be no success, because the finished design by agreement must be esteemed by both designer and client to be considered good.

In any firm, however small, you should be granted a work place. To anyone who is sensitive to the environment, as every interior designer must be, this private area—often no more than a desk—is important and should be made as pleasant as possible. However, it may become overcrowded with necessary objects and its appearance leave something to be desired.

The headquarters of an interior design firm is frequently located out of the high-rent district. However, the location must be attractive, easily accessible, safe, and not without a certain kind of prestige of its own. It is no longer possible, as in the past, to locate in a prestigious spot. Overhead costs must be whittled down to the bare bones in order to remain competitive.

With smaller space allowed for the entire firm, you, too, will have to learn to be a good space organizer and to make your station attractive on a shoestring.

At last you find yourself facing someone who seeks the kind of help that you feel capable of providing. Your first obligation is to try to interview this prospective client so as to understand and interpret his or her wants. This may take skillful effort on your part, for some people scarcely know their own needs except in the most general terms. They may talk about a place to entertain and leave you up in the air as to whether they enjoy formal dinner parties or informal gatherings.

The initial conference should include an idea of the scope of the work. Then you may suggest some similar jobs you or your firm have completed. For a really large project the client may wish to interview several firms before making a decision. If a good record has recommended your firm, you need not worry that this will cost you the job. It may make it for you.

Whatever else occurs, this first interview should establish rapport between yourself and the client. If it does not, then it is possible that something is fundamentally wrong—you, or your firm, may not be just the right partner for the undertaking. It is better to chalk up the interview to experience before more damage is done.

Your first interview may then be theoretically closed—a procedure you must learn to do decisively and graciously. Hours are worth money. By this time you should have a preliminary comprehension of the client's ideas and needs and will have promised to prepare a proposal meeting the requirements.

At this stage—or certainly after the second meeting—it has been agreed between you and your client that work will proceed. The commitment should not be postponed any later. Usually at this second meeting—or at the first if the problem is simple—you will suggest an approximate budget for the project, including a guarantee that you will receive a certain percentage of that cost, whether or not the project is accepted for completion. Such a guarantee is merely a safeguard to protect your most valuable asset as a designer—your ideas. Use of this type of guarantee differs from project to project and depends on company policy.

PROGRAMMING

Programming is compiling and organizing the data related to a project. Quite often the first step is to secure information on the location which can be in the form of an architectural plan or computer image. Three-dimensional images are often supplied by the computer, which can aid in your understanding of unconstructed space. If the project involves an architect or other professional person, such as a lighting engineer as well as an interior designer, it may be necessary to confer with that person.

You certainly will want to visit the site. In working in a visual art within a prescribed architectural framework, it is essential to fix this framework within both your visual and psychological memory. There may be aspects of the situation which only become apparent when you are on location. A visit may give you a better psychological framework from which to work.

You must verify the measurements for key positions. If some furnishing doesn't fit, possibly because some changes were made on a later set of plans which you have not received, you are nevertheless the one who is held responsible.

The second procedure, once you have a firm picture of your assignment, is to plan one or more solutions. Think through the problem until you arrive at what seems to you the most satisfactory answer. Then a second, perhaps less-expensive, scheme may likewise be plotted.

The number of presentations should not be too large for several reasons. In the first place a proliferation will simply confuse your client and yourself. This does not mean that some alterations cannot be made later, However, even these should be held to a minimum, because changes have a way of adding up and in the end may result in a hodge-podge scheme that has none of the virtue of the original. In other words, don't tinker too much with the recipe or you will finish—as the old saying goes—"with air pudding and wind sauce."

However, the real reason for not making and presenting too many proposals is the fact that as an artist the more you ponder the matter, the more certainly one plan will assert itself as the right one and will introduce the hope of acceptance. Artists, who may seem like the most pliable and amenable persons, will be found to have firm convictions at which they have arrived through much labor, and they don't easily give up their chosen notions.

Here, of course, we meet the first big paradox—you are not just an artist content to starve in a garret for your beliefs; yours is a social art, and you often have the almost impossible task of sharing a scheme which seems desirable to you with a buyer who may not be so enthusiastic.

The presentation to your client usually includes scaled floor plans with descriptions of any changes in lighting, fenestration, or permanent fixtures. Color charts, photographs of furnishings, and samples of materials for furniture, floor coverings, and window treatments are required. In many cases color renderings or 3-dimensional computer images are desirable. Occasionally there may be call for custom designing of furnishings, and preliminary drawings can be expected. However, each project must be a law unto itself with respect to the total amount of illustrative material required and warranted.

The aim of the second client conference should be to get approval and acceptance for one plan. If this is secured, you will send the client a written estimate of the costs involved. The estimate will later be carefully itemized. Obviously the preparing of such a sheet will involve your knowledge of the management and business disciplines previously mentioned.

If this proposal meets with the client's approval, a contract will be written and presented. This is, as the word implies, a legal agreement between two or several persons, each of whom must sign. Such a contract usually includes a fee payment schedule. Because much time, many orders, and money are involved in completing the project, it is customarily paid for as the work progresses, with a residual amount due on its completion.

After the contract is accepted, your time as a designer is involved in placing orders, scheduling work, supervising quality, and keeping the project running smoothly. Only when the customer is satisfied can the project be properly considered finished. As you see, you are now calling upon other skills in addition to artistry.

The above case has been described as though it were typical. In a sense it is. In another it is not. Many commitments are simpler and many are far more complicated. The latter may require many meetings, much consultation, elaborate plans, and copious cost sheets. Thus, though the renovation of a clubhouse may be considered in the private domain because it does not allow for much duplication of equipment, it could be an extensive operation.

It is this size that puts certain undertakings into the province of so-called contract work in which a larger amount of duplicating is possible. Some of this may be consigned to subcontractors. Thus, there may be some possibility of overlapping with respect to methods of operation and charging for enterprises.

DURATION OF DESIGN RELATIONS

Interior design offers a career in which it is possible to have a long-term alliance with one's clients. In this it resembles other professions such as the clerical, the medical, and the legal. This alliance results from warmhearted relations brought about by good service.

Such association is particularly characteristic of interior design in work with individual clients. Much private practice, especially that concerned with houses, is apt to be a continuing process. People speak of their designer much as they would of their attorney; satisfied, the client doesn't shop around or change.

Many dwellings are old when they are bought. Let us suppose that a family has just moved into a city. They secure a home because the schools, church, and civic facilities desired are nearby. Probably the house needs reconditioning—the walls must be brought back to prime; the floors need refinishing.

The house must be made sound before it is refurnished. Occasionally it needs serious doctoring. The entire sanitary, heating, and electrical systems may require renovating. Perhaps the exterior must be made watertight before extensive interior repairs can be made.

Although few houses call for such drastic measures, a professional interior designer should advise a client on the order of procedure and about whom to call for operations. The designer may be equipped to subcontract some of the work, such as exterior painting or interior flooring. In any case, the interior designer's opinion is valuable and trustworthy.

In some respects the program of an interior designer resembles that of a physician. Occasionally there are crises to be met; often there is only a perpetual schedule of protective and remedial care. For instance, in a house there may be a sofa which needs recovering this year or a bedroom that needs renovation another; perhaps the requirement is for a rug to place in a hall. It is important that the client be able to call on someone who has the overall picture in mind and who is competent to suggest the new so that it harmonizes with the old. This, in the long run, is money-saving for the client.

This kind of continuing planning is not limited to designing for houses. It is a large-scale operation with some designing firms. After the initial installation, say in a commercial project, the firm may contract to keep the interiors in both visual and physical repair. This sort of arrangement assures the occupants that their investment will be well maintained. This aspect of interior design is reflected in the ASID Code of Ethics: "The member agrees, whenever possible, to notify property managers, landlords, and/or public officials of conditions within a built environment that endanger the health, safety, and/or welfare of the occupants."

One type of long-term designing contract is made with the owner of a building in which spaces are leased to individual tenants. This could involve an apartment, a shopping mall, or a condominium. The lessee is placed under obligation to give all designing commissions to the one firm which has been designated. This assures the other tenants of a qualified grade of work throughout and thus protects their own equity.

Such a contract likewise safeguards the building's owner. For example, the designer may be called upon to alter a space in a mall that has been used by a men's furnishing store so that it will be suited for a good bookshop. The client who has moved into an apartment may want two suites made into one or want changes in walls, doors, or lighting. It is important to the owner of the building to know that someone who knows how to proceed will have the responsibility.

When this owner-renter policy carries into large contract work, it has often led to the designation of an architecture and interior design firm for any remodeling, each profession doing its unique type of operation. This arrangement has many advantages provided full scope and appreciation are given to the potential of each profession. It will be further detailed in the chapter on contract designing.

Many interior designers experience considerable satisfaction in being useful to people for a long period of time. Often such gratification comes from helping one family from the occasion of its first project to that later date when the children return to seek aid with their own first home.

This regard of customer for interior designer is quite genuine. It is a close and trusting relationship that results from helping others design their immediate environment. The real reward comes from being able to serve the needs, both practical and psychological, of clients so that your solution will give them pleasure through life.

TYPES OF INTERIORS WITH RESPECT TO FUNCTIONS

The types of interiors which the interior designer handles are limited only by the ability to recognize a specialized need. Whenever a problem is presented which involves the equipping of a building for its specialized function, the interior designer may be called upon to solve the attendant problems.

Although many firms are unable to specialize too closely, some remarkable particularization requiring considerable knowledge and skill does exist. For example, there is work with seacraft, aircraft, ski lodges, and vacation resorts. Schools, churches, hospitals, and stores present their special problems. Other specialties are the designing of accommodations for older citizens, day-care facilities, accommodations for the handicapped—the list is as long as the growing specialization in modern life.

Even prison facilities may be considered in need of interior design. This consideration is not with the intent of pampering the criminal. Rather, it is concerned with safety factors, with humane factors, and with the erasing of needless resentment which would eventually tend to take its toll on the public.

The designer requires imagination to see the need, brains and gumption to study a solution and the sense to see whether the idea is practical.

METHODS OF RECEIVING PAYMENT

A career should net a living. The interior designer legitimately earns this livelihood in one of several different ways. These are dependent on the nature of the task; in a complex job, several of them or a modification of one of them may be used. Each method is professionally recognized as legitimate, provided it is suited to the operation and agreed upon by the participants.

Fixed Fee

Some designers work on a fee basis. This method is particularly applicable when clients prefer to do their own purchasing. The fee must reflect the time and skill spent in advising and in writing specifications for particular products.

Often contract business is conducted on a fee basis. The design firm might plan the interiors and supply carefully detailed specs. In very large volume business, the business client may prefer to do his or her own ordering because sources of supplies are available.

Consultation Method

If there is to be no specification writing, the fee method may be referred to as the consultation method. This might be used by a school board that wishes to make its own selections and place its own contracts but wants professional advice in the planning.

Salary

Designing can be done on a strict salary basis. Large companies or syndicates, the government, architectural firms, and even some interior design firms often employ interior designers on that basis.

Retail-Wholesale Differential

Some designing service is legitimately negotiated on the basis of the difference between wholesale and retail prices. This method may be most applicable to the smaller undertakings where it may prove most understandable and convenient for the client. Or it could be used for a certain portion of the work if the client wants the designer to take full charge.

During training the interior designer is taught how to conduct business professionally. Each job presents its own requirements; in the last analysis, whatever method relates to the particular necessity should be used. In a professional undertaking the basis of charging must be clearly stated according to the best business principles; it must be understood by both designer and client, and it must be conscientiously carried out. Work of professional quality cannot be accomplished otherwise.

Custom Designing

Interior designers sometimes incur additional costs when they act as custom designers. Most major installations call for some type of custom designing. It may be a mural to be painted, a light fixture to be designed, built-in furniture to be detailed, or a rug to be woven. In such cases, the designer acts in the capacity of industrial designer and charges accordingly.

The money comes, of course, from the client and must reflect the creative talent, the labor of all sorts, and the capital involved. Management keeps these factors under control; professional ethics keeps them equitable.

TYPES OF INTERIOR DESIGN FIRMS

An interior designer has several choices in the way the business is set up: as an individually owned firm, as a partnership, as a corporation, or as a combined business with architecture. We will discuss the advantages and drawbacks of these different organizational structures.

The Individually Owned Firm

Some designers set up independent firms. In general the advice is not to take this risk until a designer has had some experience in a successfully managed concern.

What is required in the way of equipment to start solo? First, a professional designer must have a place of business, even if it is only one room in his or her home reserved exclusively for this purpose.

Then there is the need for capital, generally computed as at least the advance of six months' expenses. This money will be necessary in order to purchase samples and franchises, to meet labor costs, to set up office procedures and equipment, and to establish credit. Such expenses are incurred no matter what type of business establishment is envisaged.

An individually owned establishment has the obvious advantage of placing all control in your own hands, a precious boon if you happen to be a person with decided opinions about things aesthetic.

It is well to state, however, that an individually owned firm is one of the most risky, for there is no halving expenses if mistakes are made. The individual owner is held legally responsible for any financial losses incurred by his or her business. A later chapter more fully discusses the matter of a personally conducted interior design studio.

The Partnership

Being a member of a partnership may be a distinct advantage for the designer. Not only are expenses divided, but likewise it is often possible to gain a partner who, though with similar talents in many ways, could be a complement in others. One partner might know artistry; the other could be the business expert. Benefits would be obvious.

The drawback of a partnership is that each partner personally may be held legally responsible for the debts of the business, including those caused by other partners. The choice of a partner should thus be a prudent one.

It is well to know that a professional ranking cannot be given to a firm; it is given to and must be earned by the individual members of the firm.

The Corporation

A corporation resembles a partnership in that the people establishing it share the initial expenses and the later profits. But once established, a corporation is considered an entity unto itself; the founders personally are not legally liable for the corporation's debts. This fact reduces some of the risk associated with an individually owned business or a partnership. However, the more complex laws governing corporations may sometimes be enough of a headache to dissuade people from choosing this organizational structure.

Architectural-Interior Design Firm

A creation in comparatively recent years is the firm that is organized with both architects and interior designers as owners. It is thus equipped to offer both types of professional service. This sort of firm differs from one which is predominantly an architectural firm that hires interior designers to negotiate interior designing. In the cooperatively owned firm (frequently, though not exclusively, a family organization), both professions can practice independently, calling upon each other as needed.

Architecture-interior design firms are becoming more numerous as the realization grows that people trained in interior design have some necessary and specific knowledge that may contribute to the firm's overall effectiveness.

One needs to realize, however, that in joining such a firm—indeed in joining any specialized firm, as for instance, one dealing specifically in work with ecclesiastical buildings—one may find the course of action somewhat prescribed by the overall type of design for which the firm wishes to be noted.

THE INTERIOR DESIGNER'S SUPPLIES

The interior designer advises about and in most cases must procure a number of individual pieces of interior furnishing. One of the designer's most valuable assets—probably ranking next to artistic ability and certainly allied with it—is the knowledge of quality in supplies and of the sources from which they can be acquired. These two teamed capabilities are essential to the designer's expertise. Supplies are anything from furniture to pictures to fabrics to floor coverings. Where do these items come from, and how can one person know about them all?

Standard items such as cabinet hardware come from a wholesaler and can be ordered by number. When the commodity is less regular, the designer should examine the run of the merchandise (often known as the "line"). The designer may be helped in this by means of manufacturers' catalogues. It has become quite customary for prominent suppliers to maintain show space in what is generally known as a design center where they exhibit the best of their current offerings. Usually these showrooms are off-limits to the general public because they are for the wholesale trade. However, some design showrooms can be open to the general public, with the merchandise displayed at retail prices.

The largest design center is the Merchandise Mart in Chicago. Other excellent marts are located in the South, West, and East. New York and most other large cities present their own versions.

Although these marts run continual displays, they set aside several weeks in the spring and in the fall for presenting new products. This is the occasion when many designers visit them, as it presents an opportunity both to appraise the offerings and to attend the many special lectures given at those times.

The occasion isn't all drudgery, especially not for those who enjoy the camaraderie of meeting friends from far and near. The mart serves a real need and will probably be a part of the merchandising process for a long time to come.

The designer must know—in addition to the general furnishing mart—all the reputable sources where unique quality accessories and fine art can be found. When these objects are second-rate, the entire character of a design can be lost. It is as if one wore fine clothes and spoke ungrammatically.

This parallel emphasizes one point: expense is not a guarantee of quality, nor is the phrase "original." And, in this machine age, it is well to remember the saying "All that glitters is not gold."

THE DESIGNER'S NEED FOR SKILLED CRAFTWORKERS

Designers not only must know the commodities with which they deal, but they also have need of the services of many skilled craftworkers. Custom draperies, upholstering, and wall coverings and finishes must be expertly done. The designer should know standards of excellence and expect the best service.

Some companies are large enough that it is worth their while to have their own workshops. Occasionally these can be sublet to do work for other designers. Usually workshops are in an inexpensive district, and the building where they are located may likewise serve as a warehouse. Every designer needs a place where orders can be received and inspected before they are detailed to a client.

Workshops are generally divided into departments—possibly one for woodworking, one for textile handling, one for work with paint and wall finishes.

Because a workshop must pay its own way and be competitive with others in the field, many designers elect to use a group establishment for this service. Or they may employ independent firms and craftworkers. Such work is done on a subcontract basis so that the designer can retain responsibility and control. Whatever method of hiring is employed, it is the designer's responsibility to know and employ workers who are fully competent for the job. This is one of the designer's most important commitments.

THE HUMAN FACTOR

As an interior designer, who will be your associates? Your associates may well be a pleasant feature of your career. A good artisan who knows and takes pride in his or her work is apt to be a kindly, intelligent, friendly, and principled individual whom it is a pleasure to know. Indeed, working as an apprentice with craftworkers will allow you to know about fabrication; it will also teach much about worthwhile people.

Your suppliers, too, if properly chosen, will exhibit some of the same characteristics. The role of a good supplier figures greatly in merchandising, another important cog in the wheel of interior design. Among your suppliers you will no doubt find some of your real friends and helpers. They often can teach you much about your work and generally will respond liberally to any call for help.

You will likewise have contacts with an office staff whose efficiency is often scarcely short of phenomenal. This may be illustrated by the secretary who remembers that a client wants an order finished in time for a daughter's birthday. Considering the sheaves of statistics that pass through the office hands, there must be a corps of memory specialists or a battery of computer disks calling out the numbers.

In addition to the above worlds of craftworkers, merchandisers, and office personnel, you have a group of clients or customers. These people will probably illustrate a range of economic classes, and any pattern that may develop will undoubtedly relate to the quality of work you do and the kind of person you are. For in this, as in any other field of human endeavor, like usually attracts like.

The location of your office may likewise play its part, not so much for the aura that a prestigious location may be thought to confer, but for its convenience to desirable neighborhoods.

For instance, if your firm designs commercial interiors it may have a clientele of merchants, and the firm would probably be located in the business district. Any firm that designs for a particular ethnic group would work near where that group lives. As your work continues you will discover that the clients you most esteem will remain close to you and become in the true sense your friends.

What about your colleagues? In considering your career you would be wise to take a long, hard look at the people with whom you would be likely to associate.

Among interior designers are many of the best individuals you could wish to know in terms of interests, purposes, abilities, and character. Like artists, many of them are highly individualistic and occasionally even eccentric. Many designers have aesthetic sensitivities and yet are practical and down-to-earth in demonstrating them. They must have these two sides to their personalities in order to succeed in such a field. Some are decidedly conventional—what might be called "old guard"—in their tastes; others are more modern and innovative.

Interior designers usually are people who are alert to what is happening in the world. You can be assured that your life will never flounder in the backwaters of events. If you choose wisely, you need not hesitate about spending your days in association with the friends you will make in your chosen career.

Don't forget, however, that much depends on yourself. You will cultivate other interests, perhaps your church, your club, your museum, your political and social causes—

the list goes on and on. Your career will open, not close, doors; you must do the rest.

WORKING CONDITIONS

Regular working hours do exist in interior design. However, as in any profession, they are apt to be an illusion. What physician closes his or her desk at the end of office hours? What teacher works only during class time? Like them, interior designers must suit their schedule to the client's needs. They must prepare for and follow up their work in unscheduled hours. Even the new designer in a company will be expected to help during overtime with details such as taking inventory, assisting with rush orders, and perhaps accompanying a senior designer on a Sunday visit to a client.

Each studio has its own regulations about vacations. Customarily the so-called novice is entitled to a week's vacation with pay at the end of the first year on the job. Sometimes an extra week without pay can be arranged. The vacations, of course, grow longer and the remuneration better as time progresses.

Interior design was once a more seasonal business, the first rush being in the spring to coincide with the flurry of housecleaning. A second busy time came before the winter holidays when a freshening-up for entertaining was in order. Vacations usually filled in the gaps. However, the schedule today is unpredictable and depends largely upon when a big contract comes onto the board. The vacation may be made to coincide with a much-needed respite, or it may come as a result of some lull in assignments. Sometimes the work itself affords a trip to a foreign destination or a vacation spot. Interior design contracts today are worldwide. In fact, travel for the designer may be considered a necessity, not only to attend conventions and accept assignments in foreign places but likewise for cultural purposes.

Each studio has its own policy with regard to health insurance and other group benefits. The large professional organization, the American Society of Interior Designers (ASID), offers group health, disability, and liability insurance.

The federal government dictates the withholding of taxes and Social Security payments, regulates minimum hourly rates, mandates unemployment insurance, and to some degree specifies the physical working conditions for all employees. The design firm also may offer its own fringe benefits to increase its employees' financial well-being.

REMUNERATION

Now the big question—what about your financial reward? In earlier editions of this book we reported a range of levels which generally were quite low for the beginner to very high for the experienced designer. Talent, experience, and reputation entered into the calculation.

This situation has been somewhat changed with the entrance of large-scale contract designing. The person starting with a specialty firm does well from the beginning, and the leaders can do fabulously well.

However, the general experience is one of leveling off, with few designers earning a marginal salary and many earning substantial incomes. What interests you most: creative designing or business? If the former, and if you have any talent, you are not likely in this day and age to starve in a garret. Few who enter the profession leave it.

CHAPTER 3

YOUR SCHOOL AND YOU

STUDENT ORGANIZATIONS

At the beginning of your school life will come participation in your student chapter of the American Society of Interior Designers (ASID). This school organization and your participation in it, which automatically makes you a student member of ASID, are the important link between your school life and your professional one. Participation in the activities of a student chapter is not only a social pleasure but it also affords an opportunity to associate with the local chapter of ASID and provides access to the national scene. The ASID will take you under its wing, so to speak, and in many ways—meetings, contests, trips—you will be helped by the group of organizations concerned with professional interior design.

Not all schools have student ASID chapters. Their presence indicates a school with a quality interior design curriculum.

It is hoped that you will enjoy other extracurricular activities as well. They provide a good start for life.

EDUCATIONAL COSTS

Tuition

The cost of postsecondary education today is staggering, particularly at high-prestige private universities. Your own state university is probably the least expensive to attend. The out-of-state scholar, however, will meet expenses there about equal to those of a private college. Moreover, the nonresident student may not be admitted because of the quota basis adopted by most state schools, resulting in exclusion of any student who is not a resident of the state.

Municipal community colleges usually offer the lowest tuition. It is often possible to attend these community colleges for two years and then, if your achievement record is commendable, transfer to a four-year college or university. If your community college counselor knows this to be your intention, your courses will be so directed that you will have the minimum of credit loss in the transfer.

In preparing for this sort of move, a student should pursue a basic liberal arts curriculum while attending the community college. Specialized subjects are better reserved for the third and fourth years of study.

Tuition in two-year specialty schools, because they are generally privately owned and financed, can be high compared to community colleges. But because their offerings are not as diversified as those of four-year colleges, the costs of a specialty school can be somewhat equivalent per year.

Besides tuition, costs the student must account for include lodging, food, special fees, books, equipment, transportation, and personal expenses. These can add up quickly.

For many reasons, it is not always wise to think in terms of the most expensive school, presuming it to be the best. If your own financial status is limited, overreaching may court economic disaster. On the other hand, it is never wise to skimp on a good education for the sake of a few dollars. It may be possible to obtain the extra money in some legitimate way, and it may well be worth the trouble.

Your guidance counselor can be of help in learning the exact costs for attendance at a particular school. These not only fluctuate from school to school and location to location but with the present rate of inflation are always rising.

Personal Expenses

The same kind of logic can be applied to your personal expenses. They are a matter of individual discretion. Some thrift may well be advisable, but too much may deprive you of valuable contacts and experiences. Good living conditions are one guarantee of health; it costs to be sick. Moreover, the toll for conditions which may tax your moral stamina could be the near-destruction of a life.

You cannot do good work without good equipment. Label it, keep it in good repair, and guard it. If you are careless with your property, it may be lost or even stolen.

Expense for extracurricular activities and for travel may need to be minimal. If possible, arrange to go on educational field trips. However, there will always be future opportunities if you can't stretch your dollars for the present ones.

Basic student wardrobe needs are not necessarily expensive. A few campus changes, an informal business ensemble that can be dressed up or down, and some simple outfits for social activities are all that are absolutely necessary. Designer-labeled clothing is popular, but it also is one of the more expendable items in a tight budget.

However, you should guard against a certain provincialism in dressing. The career you have chosen is one where what is termed "good taste" is very important. You will need to have regard for it in your later business life. One purpose of the kind of education you are seeking is to obtain a vision of what is appropriate behavior and dress for a professional. Sometimes there are other standards than the one that is right under your nose, and though every young person wishes to match peers in matters of dress, there are codes of dressing—of neatness, cleanliness, and appropriateness—that have not been discarded.

FINANCIAL AID

While the last part of the twentieth century may be remembered as one where educational costs got out of hand, it likewise fares well to be remembered as one of the periods when there was the most available aid. Although such assistance is related to economics, it no longer is accessible only to those who have great financial need. The funds are now available to help the exceptional scholar.

Every kind of help depends upon keeping an acceptable scholastic average. Moreover, aid may be secured in a number of different ways. It may take the form of scholarships, loans, grants, or employment opportunities.

School-administered scholarships are apt to be limited, although some special scholarships are frequently negotiated through such agencies as religious organizations, labor unions, ethnic societies, and civic groups.

A similar statement can be made regarding loans. A loan, of course, is offered with the legal requirement of repayment at some time in the future, usually following graduation. It should not be overlooked that many commercial loan companies—indeed many banks—offer their services to both parents and students. The government likewise may be a good source.

Grants, which do not require repayment, are sometimes awarded to students with exceptional financial need or to those who give promise of exceptional academic excellence. Some of these grants are negotiated through the government.

Most schools offer some form of school-affiliated employment that is available to those with the proper credentials. Such jobs often are limited in number and highly sought-after by students.

Colleges generally conduct a student financial aid program. Through such a program, the various sources for obtaining financial help are centralized. You apply to the financial aid office of the college to which you are (or hope to be) accepted. The people in this office will help you prepare the papers necessary for application. It is indeed surprising how, with directed effort, the doors of education can be opened to the deserving student.

Start this kind of financial aid request early. More often than not there is a considerable time lag between application and acceptance. Do not give up too easily—persistence often pays off.

A final word is in order. Many students who might well profit by and contribute benefits to higher education may never reach their goal simply because there has been no one to help them make arrangements for going on for further education. While the high school graduate is urged to take the initiative for his or her own future, there may be need for someone to provide that little encouragement that the transition requires. There is no more rewarding task than that of helping the young find their opportunities.

SELECTING A SCHOOL

For most people the selection of a school is based first on economics. What school can you afford? The school that will permit you to live at home while studying is generally the least expensive, and the one farthest from home the most expensive if only by reason of the costs of transportation to and from the campus.

There are, of course, other matters besides the money to be considered. Is the school situated in a metropolitan area or in a small town? Is the school complex so large that it becomes a city in itself, as may be the case with some state university campuses?

Some arguments favor a small institution. If you have never been far from home, it may be easier to make the transition to independence within the confines of a more intimate campus. It is possible to become lost in the big school to the extent of not making adequate contact with your fellow students. However, the laboratory groupings that are common to interior design programs favor a genuine feeling of camaraderie, thereby making isolation less of a problem.

The city campus has some advantages. Working opportunities, particularly in interior design, are probably better in an urban area. At design centers you will gain firsthand acquaintance with supply sources, and you will see outstanding examples of design. It will be possible for you to observe various aspects of the work, which may help you decide which interests you most. When schools are not located in cosmopolitan areas, field trips are usually planned to provide some of these opportunities.

Another plus for the metropolitan setting is its proximity to museums and centers for the performing arts. One of the strongest points in favor of interior design as a professional study is the fact that it spurs cultural study by its students and practitioners. The stimulus for appreciating the world of the cultural arts is everpresent. You will find that you have grown in your ability not only to understand fine art but also to make critical decisions about environmental art. A study of quality in one art helps in the understanding of another.

Some schools feature a term of foreign travel or a semester in a foreign school as part of their curriculum. Such a semester, well planned and well guided, can be of inestimable worth in broadening your horizons.

Be certain that the school you choose has earned a favorable academic rating. Write for its catalog, and study the descriptions of its courses. It is not a bad idea to piece together a summary of the work the school will expect you to do. It is true that you select your goal, but your school determines your path.

The school will ask for your credentials before considering your admission. In addition to your character reference (be certain to both ask permission for this and write a thank-you letter to anyone who has done you the favor of writing one), most schools require a transcript of your high school academic record. A grade level equivalent to a "C" is necessary for admission to many state colleges, and many private institutions require a higher level.

The subjects that you take in high school must include a prescribed minimum of academic courses. The old rule of ranking in the upper one-third of your high school graduating class still holds true for admission to many colleges and universities. This rule, even where it is no longer in effect, helps you to evaluate your capability in relation to the school in which you hope to enroll. It is well enough to aim high; perhaps it makes better sense not to try to go to a school where you know that your chances of real success against the rest of the student body are small. A school that challenges your capabilities but does not strain them is best.

Your high school advisor has probably told you about certain tests you will have to take before admission to a four-year college or university. Chief of these are the American College Test (ACT) and the Scholastic Aptitude Test (SAT). Achievement tests in special subjects may likewise be requested. Two- and three-year schools generally are not as rigid in their admission requirements.

When considering your future scholastic home, take time if possible to visit the campus. Talk to former and present students to find out whether the atmosphere is one you will enjoy. What about the social life offered? Is it within your means and to your liking? Although there is a good deal to be said for experiencing ways of life beyond your usual paths, it is not wise to break with the first years of your life too broadly in the beginning. Church affiliations should be considered. What about living conditions? Both deserve attention in this age of changing mores.

After careful thought, send in your application to a limited number of schools; three should be enough. It costs both the school and you to process your papers. Concentrate on the idea of getting your top choice, but with a cushion provision should your first selection fail. If you do not receive permission for entrance to any of the schools you have chosen, don't give up. Maybe some technical error is accountable. Try some other schools, carefully ensuring that you have scrupulously complied with the admission directions. It is important to watch details.

A WORD OF ADVICE

This advice is offered with full realization that each generation of scholars faces its own climate and will—and must—make its own decisions. Don't jeopardize your vocation for the sake of excessive interim employment unless it is absolutely necessary.

When in school you will have completed about 30 to 34 credit hours per year. In this arrangement, one class hour plus two study or laboratory hours per week for a four-month term equals one credit hour in academic units. This amounts to five eight-hour days per week or forty to fifty clock hours per week in academic pursuits. Additional work at a part-time job may endanger your academic standing, undermine your health, or deprive you of friendly sociability. Estimate your capabilities; do not overextend yourself. It would probably be better to arrange some sort of financial aid and pay it back when your rate of income will be higher.

Become involved in and develop a sense of loyalty and responsibility to your professional group. No profession can be stronger than its members. While giving of yourself you develop that sense of allegiance to something bigger than yourself, which is the keynote to success in the richest sense of the word.

Many schools are located where museums, orchestras, and theaters are convenient. Sometimes working as a guide or usher will pay your way to performances. It is only through individual effort that one becomes a person of imagination and vision.

Read as you can—and along with your favorite books of whatever character, learn to write. Interior design is a ripe field. Just remember what the great architects did for their profession through writing.

Likewise learn to know your fellow students. They, or those like them, will be your world. If you have reservations, then maybe you had best think twice about any profession you have chosen—or about yourself.

Your school years will be all too short a span; you will not accomplish half of what you had hoped to do. Place your foot firmly on the first step; the second will be easier. Enjoy your climb. Have the kind of fun that comes from pride in your work, respect for yourself, and the kind of regard for the world that accompanies a perspective which keeps you from thinking you are its center. Keep alert, keep thinking, and keep flexible.

CHAPTER 4

EDUCATIONAL AND PERSONAL REQUIREMENTS

We are now at the place where we will assume that you have considered interior design as a career. You have accepted the proposition that it is both an art and a science, a business and a profession. We have delved a bit into the intricacies of interior design practice. At present we are concerned with what you must do to be eligible to become an interior designer.

Perhaps no more than 20 years ago you need have done little more to be considered an interior designer than hang out your shingle and fulfill certain minor requirements, such as the securing of a civic license to practice and the annexing of certain sample lines to show to your clients.

Such easy facility is largely a thing of the past. In 17 states and the District of Columbia, you must obtain the legal right to practice under the title of interior designer. This privilege usually requires the passing of a state examination and the guarantee of an education of prescribed quality. Be sure to check the laws of the state in which you intend to practice your profession.

The profession itself makes its requirements through its organizations, which will be discussed in greater detail in Chapter 9.

HIGH SCHOOL PREPARATION

A high school diploma or its equivalent is customarily required for entrance to any school qualified to give the interior design training needed for professional status.

If you are attending a technical high school at the present time, possibly you can take some course work in art or woodworking or fabric construction that will give you a taste for subjects that you will meet in your later education. Word processing and computer skill should be mastered whenever it is available. They are nearly essential for students and professionals today.

If you are attending an academic high school, these same suggestions are valid. A college preparatory program will be advised by your counselor if it is known that you intend to enter a four-year college or university.

Whatever your future plans, it is best to spend your high school years obtaining a good scholastic foundation. Training in the fundamentals of the English language is indispensable. With interior design growing fast in international prominence, it is wise to begin the study of a foreign language and to miss no chance to become proficient in it.

Beginning mathematics is necessary for all sciences, and it is probably true that the subject is more easily mastered when one is young. You could likewise begin your study of history and political science.

Social life and sports are good, too. They will serve you well throughout life. But they should never come at the expense of that high school diploma, which is your first ticket of admittance to a future career.

THE STATE OF EDUCATION

Types of Schools

A number of different types of schools teach various aspects of interior design. There is now in progress a concerted effort on the part of the profession to group these schools into categories based on the length of their programs, the nature of their curricula, and their ultimate purposes. The types of schools in existence will be discussed later in this chapter.

Toward Some Standardization

Interior design has proved so popular a subject in so many schools and colleges above the secondary school level that there are few institutions of higher learning that do not offer a group of subjects focused in this direction.

This rather casual state of affairs prompted the Interior Design Educators Council (IDEC) to make a critical study of the situation. The study, under the direction of Professor Arnold Friedmann of the University of Massachusetts, concentrated not only on curricula but likewise on school administration and physical facilities. After this study several important changes were made.

In the first place and most importantly, the study proposed that a formal accrediting body be formed. This body is now known as the Foundation for Interior Design Education Research (FIDER). Formed in 1970, FIDER contains representatives from concerned professional organizations and is recognized by the Council on Postsecondary Accreditation of the U.S. Department of Education. However, it is a nongovernmental organization.

Today, FIDER accredits interior design programs at three- and six-year intervals. It must be emphasized that FIDER accredits interior design programs and not the schools offering interior design. Therefore, the fact that a school is not accredited by FIDER does not necessarily mean that it is not offering a good program.

Today in the United States and Canada, more than 500 schools and universities offer curricula in interior design, 108 of which are accredited by FIDER.

FORMAL EDUCATION: ITS CONTENT

Career Courses

What are the subjects in an interior design curriculum that are suited to training for the profession? If all the recommended ones were to be included, the school term could easily extend to the seven years that characterize the training for the professorial rank. With the phenomenal cost of education today, it is fanciful to expect that many could or would consider such an expenditure of either time or money.

The various disciplines inherent in interior design were suggested in Chapter 1. Here we consider them with respect to curricula. These subjects may be found in a school catalog under a variety of titles. Read the course descriptions carefully—if they are available—in order to understand the content.

Although it is undesirable to overregiment courses of study because schools can frequently have acceptable and unique offerings, nevertheless some consideration should be given to standardizing curricula if for no other purpose than to facilitate transfer of credit from one institution to another.

The subjects you will study in a professional curriculum usually are divided into two classes. First come those that are essential for specialized training in interior design. By agreement between educators, these subjects comprise over half the credit hours available in a four-year curriculum. They constitute your major. The shorter the total course of study, the more prescribed the major offering will have to be in order to insure knowledge of the fundamentals.

Looking back to Chapter 1, it is clear that these required subjects relate to skills, appreciation, and information that the interior designer should possess upon graduation.

Noncareer Courses

Again glancing back to Chapter 1, you will note that one capability of an interior designer we mentioned has not been specifically prescribed in the career courses. It is the discipline which customarily is said to provide cultural understanding.

After providing for the necessary professional subjects, what about the amount of time left for the knowledge and comprehension of the culture of the world in which the designer will practice? Is there enough available time for accomplishing this?

We are now talking about that part of the education of an interior designer which helps him or her design so as to help people. To be able to do this, any professional person—whether doctor, minister, architect, or writer—must understand both the world and the people who live in it.

Without belaboring the matter, this means the inclusion of the humanities, or liberal arts—pure science, economics, language and literature, history, philosophy or logic, religion, the social sciences, and the arts, including music.

These liberal arts subjects are what Professor Jerome S. Bruner of Harvard, in his little book *On Knowing,* calls "exercises for the left hand," because they are not directly concerned with beating out the measure of daily living. Rather, they shape the quality of a life much as the directions from the orchestra leader's left hand create the quality of the music.

These liberal arts subjects, if carefully chosen and wisely taught, are absolutely essential to the profession of interior design. If neglected in a curriculum or in the prescription for the training of interior designers, the profession as a profession is doomed. Culture with a capital "C" is something more than a thin veneer, and in a very real sense this characteristic should mark the interior designer.

The liberal arts subjects should bring you pleasure; they will likewise enable you to see backwards and forwards in time, broadly in space, and deeply in human motivation. These are distinctions that the interior designer, along with other professional people who serve humanity, must have and forever strive to improve.

In most colleges the liberal arts subjects are divided into groups as previously indicated, and the student is required to select a basic number of credit hours from each of several groups so that his or her outlook will not be too restricted.

It has often been found that the average student, if given a choice, will select the easiest courses, the fad courses, the courses that do not presuppose a supportive framework. But it is your money and your time; don't be so foolish with it. Search out those subjects that are fundamental. For example, take math before physics. This is the only way to master the material and go on to conquer courses in structure and design. Take ancient history or a survey history course before one dealing with the eighteenth century; take English before French; make sure sociology precedes a course in unemployment relief. If you have the basics you will find that you can—and will—master new knowledge over the years. Don't end up with a potpourri that has no distinct flavor.

All this might be called the "bedrock" theory of interior design education. Buy wisely. You can thus become a truly professional person and will be respected as such.

KINDS OF PROGRAMS

One objective way to categorize schools is by time bracket—the length of time, based on a full schedule, necessary to obtain a certificate or a diploma. The following classification of schools with design programs has been established by the Foundation for Interior Design Research (FIDER).

Certificate Programs

Some schools offer a program of at least two years' duration which results in the awarding of a certificate upon successful completion. These preprofessional programs are generally found in technical institutes. The emphasis in their curricula is in training for positions other than professional interior design. These positions include drafter, illustrator, specification writer, office administrator, or support person to interior designers.

This type of school is not accredited for teaching professional interior design. The program of this type of school is called "terminal." Most often none of its credits are applicable toward a degree in a school offering professional credit.

Four-Year Professional or Baccalaureate Programs

The title here is self-explanatory. The graduate of such a curriculum is academically qualified to become a professional interior designer. Four- or five-year programs are offered as major fields of specialization in a great many universities and are quite equal to state institutions.

The school in which such a major is offered must grant a baccalaureate (bachelor's) degree, and the major must place emphasis on training for professional interior design. The curriculum is planned to serve the needs of the interior design profession in their broadest definition. In addition to the skills particular to interior design, the curriculum should likewise afford the opportunity for study in the humanities.

After completing such an education, young designers must obtain some practical experience before they can be considered full-fledged professional interior designers. The time requirement for this experience is dependent upon such factors as the talent, dedication, and opportunity of the individual. Candidates for professional status must likewise pass the examination given under the auspices of the National Council for Interior Design Qualification (NCIDQ).

Postgraduate Interior Design Programs

Such a program generally involves at least 30 semester hours of credit beyond a bachelor's degree for a master's degree and 90 postgraduate semester hours for a doctorate. These graduate degrees must be obtained from schools that offer degrees in subjects other than interior design.

In addition to their academic standing, prospective students for advanced degrees must produce evidence of their creative design ability before they are allowed to matriculate. They should likewise indicate high promise of success in postgraduate interior design study. The courses intended for the curriculum for graduate work must be especially so marked. The program should necessitate either rigorous academic research or highly creative design. It should include a dissertation worthy of publication.

FIDER does not accredit postgraduate interior design programs. IDEC publishes a listing of postgraduate interior design programs which may be obtained by writing IDEC.

As a postscript, it must be stated that no correspondence course can be credited toward professional interior design.

YOUR QUALIFICATIONS

Physical Traits

Good health and stamina are definite assets. You will sometimes work, often under strain, for long and unpredictable hours. Customers must be interviewed at their convenience. You cannot sit in an ivory tower—much of your time will be spent away from headquarters. You will have to drive many places and perhaps carry many things. (All of this is less true if you are a member of a company with a large, centralized office.)

There are subcontractors to be met and shopping to be done. At times you work in buildings that are under construction. Travel will be part of your life. In short, you will be a very active person. Good health and physical endurance will help you to enjoy the practice of interior design.

Feeling well and liking your work will give you a start toward making a good appearance. You need not be beautiful or handsome or have the charisma of a movie star. In fact, that kind of glamour might unflatteringly suggest an overpowering concern with your own image. Yet you should try to preserve those outward signs of good health: clear skin and fit figure. You should have well-cared-for hands and hair.

Your attire requires special attention because it does have some bearing on your success. Interior designers are very busy people, and their clothes must be able to stand the pace. If you customarily give forethought to your wardrobe, making it suitable to a way of life, you will readily adapt to your new business needs.

However, business is not school, and you will have to exert yourself to observe how to dress in your new situation. A good rule is that when in doubt about clothing for special occasions, dress simply rather than ornately. Your clothes do matter, but if they are neat and in keeping with conventional taste and if they have that attractiveness which your artistry can suggest, they will indicate a person of intelligence and sincerity rather than one of high fashion. You want to be taken seriously, and your clothes shouldn't detract from that goal.

Personality Traits

Personality is a very strange thing, intimately linked to factors that are part physical, part intellectual, and certainly part emotional. We use the term *personality* to describe the set of characteristic reactions to the external world that are unmistakably yours.

First, your attitude toward personal behavior is important. What is the set of values by which you guide your life? On one level this concerns your attitude toward social conventions and etiquette. Although we have just passed through a period of change in social customs which is quite phenomenal, you will find that the meaningful portions of the old codes are still revered. The good manners that spring from consideration for others are never out of style and always mark superiority. If for no other reason, civility is only good common sense and certainly is good business.

You, as a designer, will encounter new and perhaps strange customs in your travels. You will meet many different kinds of people with varying economic, social, and educational backgrounds. Basic good breeding will help you to discern and act upon ways other than those to which you have been accustomed. It might be wise to secure a standard and reliable book of etiquette to consult when faced with the need to accommodate to a group with whose customs you are unfamiliar.

Related to all the foregoing is a genuine liking for people. Interior design, perhaps more than many others, is a social profession. The interior designer should be to a certain extent gregarious. This does not mean that he or she would be unhappy when alone. Such a situation would suggest an absence of personal resourcefulness. But neither can the designer shrink from contact with the world.

The interior designer must meet and come to know many people, must try to discern their needs and wants. As Isamu Noguchi, the famous sculptor, furniture designer, and landscape architect said, "Interior design is a continual seminar."

Also essential for the interior designer is that quality known as tact. This is the ability to handle a situation so as to increase the stature of another without diminishing your own.

Cheerfulness is another good quality to possess in this as in any field. It is particularly appropriate to the designer because it is the basis for a positive and optimistic approach to problems. So many unforeseeable annoyances will occur. Delays or mistakes in orders, exasperating indecision on the part of customers, or a judgment of your own that you later regret—all of these troubles must be met and handled. You will need a guiding philosophy in which cheerfulness and patience and thoughtfulness are partners.

Industriousness and dependability are required for any job. From somewhere must come the strength to carry on when the spirit and body are weak. These characteristics are linked closely to the creativity that a designer must have. For the present let us call it initiative. You will generally be your own master. You will need that determination and self-discipline to lift yourself out of apathy and force yourself to create at your top performance level. This is the drive to put imagination to work.

Next we come to a personality characteristic which is difficult to analyze but which is of greatest importance. It is the ability to lead, to convince others that your solutions are worth accepting. In school organizations to which you belong, do friends seek your advice? Do they listen to you when you speak? Do you somehow become a symbol to rally around? There may be various degrees and kinds of leadership, but you must have some of it. Your professional training will help to augment that which you do possess. If you feel that you do not have leadership capabilities, then perhaps some of the interior design areas that place less importance on this quality would be a wiser and more satisfying choice for you.

And now we come to the last and most important personality trait you will need to become a successful interior designer—moral stamina. This quality and the need for it do not change with time. It means, in the present context, that almost involuntarily you cling to two basic ethical principles: honesty and fairness. The interior design profession has an ethical code in which honesty in conducting your own business and fairness in respect to your dealings with others are basic principles. Such a code cannot be an occasional cause for observance. It must come first in all that you do. And, when necessary, it must be clearly expressed.

Mental Traits

Psychologists debate the relationship between mentality and personality. However, the two can be separated for purposes of analysis.

You need not be academically superior, but you would do well to discipline yourself to be analytical and orderly in your thinking. These qualities of mind alone may be sufficient to help you up the scholastic ladder. Nor do these qualities run counter to aesthetic sensitivity; in fact, they may be the wellspring from which creative art flows. You must be organized in your thoughts in order to create art. It is probably true that when the artist is most wildly driven, his or her impulses and thoughts possess an innate order of which he or she alone is conscious.

Your mind should be keen and alert—awareness is a good name for this quality. Awareness is the capacity to bring life into sharp focus. You are much in need of this quality as you strive to see into the lives of others.

Of intellectual skills, you must be able to speak and write correctly and interestingly. And your voice should be well-modulated. Although we assume that, having come from a good secondary school education, you possess these necessary attributes, nevertheless a word of caution may be tendered. Avoid all the lazy expressions that surround you.

This doesn't mean that you must be priggish in your speech; it does mean that you should not let yourself fall victim to sloppy and careless phrases, such as "you know." Good language skills are so taken for granted that they are scarcely given the praise they deserve. However, poor speaking, rightfully or not, has a pernicious ability to brand you irredeemably.

Artistic Talent

Many students ask if they need artistic talent in order to become interior designers. Of course, the answer is "yes." In fact, artistic talent is as necessary for the good interior designer as for the good painter, sculptor, or musician. In addition, the interior designer needs an uncommon amount of intuitive sensitivity to the needs of others.

How do you estimate the artistic ability that is necessary? Check these requisites—good eyesight, a steady hand, and adequate training in drafting and rendering. It is beneficial to have hands that feel, ears that hear, and even a nose that smells in order to create in a medium that uses all of the senses. Interior design makes sensitive use of space, shape, color, light, and visual texture. Add to it, through the use of touch, sound, and smell, that richness of expression which our culture is rapidly losing. Incorporate in your designs the materials you love to touch, sounds you love to hear, and some enticing odors. What about a cashmere throw, a striking clock, and spicy pine?

And the fifth, the muscular sense? All visual rhythm and balance depend on it. Do you love to play ball? To dance? To ride?

Are you concerned about the appearance and appeal of your surroundings? Do you respond emotionally as well as intellectually to them? Do you feel the need to create good art through them? It is your need to create in this medium that is the first measure of your artistic ability.

BUSINESS POTENTIAL

This necessary ability is, for our purposes, divided into two parts. First: your sales ability. It is necessary if your prized ideas are to see the light of day. You can never produce your kind of art in a garret and on a little less than a shoestring. Many, therefore, maintain that you should relish the competition and excitement of the marketplace with its dictates of maximum profit and an accompanying selling style. The profession of interior design does not subscribe to this. Good selling is to be able to communicate the quality in your designing so that it will be seen by your client as well as by yourself. Selling of this sort is professional, and it is necessary.

Look this commercial aspect of interior design squarely in the eye. If it is distasteful to you, try to enter the interior design field as an assistant or possibly in one of its educational phases. However, if you like to create, to sell your product, to see it rise into actuality, then enter the practicing arena, where there will be reward in personal satisfaction as well as in tangible assets.

Selling, of course, is only one part of the business picture. The second part is shrewd business sense. If you are so much the creator that all thought of business is an irksome interruption, then by all means hire someone to help you with financial management. Such added expense must be made to pay its own cost.

You will receive business training during your school years. Gain the necessary comprehension of the subject. This will help you understand how important it is to run the establishment with a tight rein.

But don't kill a good artist for a poor businessperson. Learn what is necessary to gain a fair profit, work hard enough to guarantee it, and watch carefully that it is not allowed to slip through your fingers.

Last, but not least, as an addendum to your physical, personal, intellectual, and business qualifications, we add one which permeates your attitude toward all. This is an outlook that incorporates a mature sense of humor. Without it you can be a sorry soul indeed, and your creations, your chances of bringing them to life and of giving any joy and satisfaction to your clients, are slim.

CHAPTER 5

GETTING STARTED—EMPLOYMENT

WHERE TO APPLY

The first place to apply is the school placement office, which should have information regarding the opportunities for employment in your field. The placement service has worked with your major department to learn where such opportunities exist and to promote the applications of qualified candidates.

The placement counselor will want personal interviews with you. Tips on how to interview successfully will follow later in this chapter.

If you have in mind a quite definite geographic location where you wish to work, then secure a listing of the professional interior designers in that area. A limited list of these is procurable from the yellow pages of the local phone book.

If your seeking a position requires that you apply at a distance from your home or school, it is advisable that you have sufficient funds to live for a time in the locality where you expect to work. Not only is it advantageous to be available for consultation by the employer, but if you contract for the job, you may need funds for living until your first paycheck comes. You have already spent much on your education; don't shortchange yourself for lack of a small cost.

Perhaps you will not need to apply. If you have already acquitted yourself well as a student assistant with some firm and if you wish to remain with it, your immediate future may be secure. You may enter the firm as a junior designer.

EXPERIENCE REQUIREMENT

Experience of having worked in the field seems to be a universal requirement. How can you give a record of experience if this is your first try?

From an employer's point of view, the question is understandable. Although a good apprentice, assistant, aide, or technician can relieve the office of much of the work tedium, a poor one can be a liability. He or she can misfile necessary documents and materials, may seem always to be absent at the most critical times, or will ask too many questions about problems that a little observation or common sense should have solved. He or she cannot be trusted to take over some elements of the work and to perform them well. By the time the novice has learned regimen, capability, and responsibility within a particular firm, much time and money may have been lost. Therefore, a prospective employer is anxious to know something of your previous work record.

Some schools include a learning experience out in the field during the term of study. Sometimes it is experienced as summer work. This may be a requirement of the course of study even though no time can be allotted to it during the school year.

If a full-time position with an interior design establishment is not available, what other types of employment could you seek that would chalk up the needed requisite of experience?

The novice interior designer has little trouble getting part-time work. He or she has something to sell. Drafting skills, model making ability, CAD knowledge, color expertise, furnishing interests, sales skills—all may be used by an employer on a short-term basis.

The opportunities are myriad. Some beginning designers gain positions in showrooms of firms dealing in fine furnishings. Others work in department stores. Both locations give good initial experience. You can learn about carpets, curtains, wall coverings, furniture and accessories, and, in some situations, about antiques. You can scarcely help learning much about selling.

You might first work with paint and wallpaper companies, furniture manufacturers, lumber outlets, real estate companies, building contractors, office supply houses, and even credit departments. Properly understood, each can bring grist to your mill. Recreational environments—camp counseling, tutoring, sports participation—also can teach something about the world of intercommunications. Emphasize this aspect when applying for an interior design opportunity.

If the work is away from your home base, it may be valuable in giving you a broader outlook on how others live. An interior designer should not have a provincial outlook.

Many designers have said that they wished that students had more experience with interior design trades. If such are not included in your school's curriculum, work for a time in a slipcover and drapery workshop or in one refinishing or upholstering furniture. Woodworking, wall finishing, carpet installation—a knowledge of these techniques learned in a shop with high standards can help you in your later work.

If you plan to enter the contract field, it might be advisable to seek computer work in the company of a contract designer. You will discover that there exist so many specializations in the interior design field that it is advisable, if you have a liking for some particular one, to begin directing your talents early.

APPLYING FOR POSITIONS

Begin to think about your application for permanent work no later than your last year of study. Gather all of your personal data for easy presentation.

This collection of data will include what is known as your portfolio. A portfolio is in reality a showing of the best work you have done over your academic years. As its compilation is frequently one of the academic requirements of your senior year and as the interior design profession is at work setting certain standards for it, no more will be said about it here. Mention of it is, for the sake of summary, made in the following account of a resume.

THE RESUME

It is wise to prepare this record well in advance of any interview. You should have it typed and keep several copies. Generally speaking, today's student will prepare the resume on a computer and keep it for retrieval on a disk. Of course it should be dated and revised whenever necessary. The resume should be concisely written and, if possible, fit entirely on one page. It should include at least the following information:

- *Introductory information*

  Name, address, and phone number.

  (Do not include age, height, weight, marital status, race, religion, or other such personal information.)
- *Type of position sought*

  Describe in terms of job requirements, skills, and personal characteristics.
- *Education*

High school: name, place, dates of attendance, major courses.

Advanced schooling: name, place, date of graduation, or number of years attended, courses of study with brief description of content.

Academic record: usually a transcript from the school. You can obtain it from the school office.

- *Experience*

  Position, type of experience, dates, reasons for both accepting and leaving.
- *Social and professional organizations and experiences*
- *Further personal information*

  Special hobbies or interests, travel, social service.
- *References*

  Character reference, perhaps from a former employer, a teacher, a member of the clergy, or a long-time personal friend. (Be sure to ask permission for this courtesy and to express your thanks for it.) On the resume, you may simply state, "References available upon request." Be prepared to supply at least three if your prospective employer asks.
- *Portfolio*

  This should not be shown unless requested. It is becoming increasingly important for interior designers to have samples of their work, preferably shown in 8″ × 10″ glossy photographs. Some schools request that both a resume and photographs of work be assembled in the senior year.

Accompanying your resume is a cover letter. This letter explains why you are sending along the resume and gives you the opportunity to emphasize in greater detail the aspects of your experience and personality that most strongly correlate to the specific position for which you are applying.

Address your letter to the person in charge of employment, making certain that the name and title are correct. (If you are unsure, a secretary at the company will often be glad to supply you with the correct information.) Keep your dictionary open and check on the spelling of any doubtful words. The letter should be typed on clean, white bond paper or business stationery. You may choose to include a stamped, self-addressed return envelope for reply, but this is not mandatory.

Letters should convey their message in logical order. Begin by stating your purpose for writing: "I would like to apply for a position as . . ." Give any specific information that will clarify the statement, such as "I understand that your design assistant has just resigned," or "When you were on our campus, you suggested that we write to you when our graduation date drew near."

Follow this with a statement about what you think your contribution to the firm could be: "I have had extensive training in CAD (computer aided design) and believe my skills would be an asset to Acme Design," or "I have had considerable experience with boating, and I believe I could be valuable to the firm's contract division which handles transportation designing." If possible, quantify your experience; "90 hours of carpentry training" sounds more impressive than the vague "much experience in carpentry."

Make a statement about the enclosure of your resume. Avoid repeating any facts that appear there. However, it is not amiss to call attention by means of further explanation to important items that you believe would be to your particular advantage: "You will note that I have worked during the summers for XYZ Department Store. During that time, I was promoted from sales clerk to assistant manager of carpet sales." Be as specific as you can about your accomplishments. The better they speak for themselves, the less you will seem to be blowing your own horn.

Having stated your qualifications, it is appropriate to request an interview. Allow the other person to name the time and place. If it is possible for you to go to the location during one of your vacation periods, mention this. However, it should be left to the prospective employer to make the final decision. Remember that you are the applicant and are not the one to call the shots. Conclude with a restatement of your purpose in a slightly different but clear, concise way.

If you are granted an interview, follow your first letter with a note of acknowledgement confirming that you will be present for the appointment at such-and-such a time and place. If there is no answer to your first letter and if you wish to do so, you might follow up with a second note stressing some points that you had not emphasized before. Use your own judgment about this. Sometimes it works to your advantage, but occasionally an employer is irked by such persistence.

After an interview, a simple thank-you note is in order. Good public relations is the art of politeness and consideration in dealing with others. Even though your writing may be of no personal benefit, you are a representative of your school and an example of its training. The thank-you note also indirectly reminds the prospective employer of your continued interest in the job.

Some believe that a telephone call or a personal visit is more effective than a letter when requesting an interview. The theory seems to be that it is more difficult for an employer to give a negative answer to a person than to a letter. This is a matter of opinion and a question of circumstances. It is more professional to write. The important thing is to request an interview on the terms of the employer rather than to appear unannounced.

A word of final advice: Names and titles are of great importance. Learn such, for instance, about the person to whom you should address your letter. Be certain to memorize the name, to spell and pronounce it correctly, to use it whenever the occasion arises, and to make use of the proper title whenever it is applicable.

THE INTERVIEW

Sooner or later an employment interview is necessary. Many students seem apprehensive of this and regard it as something to be dreaded. There is really no cause for such anxiety. Most firms are eager to learn of fresh new talent even if they are unable to hire more employees at the time. Many advisors say that the interview is a good experience even if it does not result in immediate employment. Practice can bring poise and confidence.

The mental approach should be one of assurance; be as calm, poised, and hopeful as possible. As part of the technique, try to get a good night's rest and eat an adequate breakfast. Never take a negative point of view or advertise your weak points. In other words, don't parade your fear of failure.

There is just no substitute for an interest in the position you are seeking. You must convey your faith in the ability to cope with its responsibilities. If you really feel that the work is beyond your capabilities, say so without underselling or overrating yourself.

Be certain to be prompt. Allow all necessary time for delays in transportation. Put your best foot forward in posture, voice, diction, and business dress.

Do not be surprised if your interviewer asks you a number of questions that seem unrelated to the matter at hand. The interviewer may ask what books you have read recently, what plans you have for your future, what kind of music you prefer. You are being tested on some of the intangibles of your personality, qualities which are of importance to a wise employer in this field. Minor skills can be learned more easily than personalities can be altered.

Answer these questions frankly, simply, and directly. Be honest, but above all be affable and gracious. If being yourself and flying your own colors is not going to count, then you will be better off without the position. You must fit or the situation will be untenable.

During the interview you will want to learn some things about the work. If the information is not volunteered, ask. You have a right to know about the organization and what you can expect from it. You, too, are interested in intangibles. It is better to learn these direct from headquarters than attempt to probe that always dubious means of the grapevine. However, do not ask about such details as medical benefits or vacation time; these are best reserved for a second meeting. Confine your questions to the job itself.

Your specific knowledge about phases of interior design may be inquired about; you may even be asked to answer some questions to test your competency or to do some drawing of a design nature. However, today, the portfolio presentation usually substitutes for this.

AFTER THE INTERVIEW

It is important to terminate an interview before you have taken up too much of a busy executive's time. In fact, although it is not desirable to talk too little, neither should you overtalk. As one applicant said, "I suddenly realized that I had the job in the bag if I would just keep quiet."

When you leave, express your appreciation for the interview and your wish (if at this time you have one) that the outcome may be favorable. It might be suitable to ask whether you should make any further inquiry about the matter.

If you have convinced the potential employer about your ability to handle the work and your suitability for the particular situation, you have added to the positive side of your ledger whatever the specific outcome. One interviewer was so favorably impressed by a candidate that, although there was no opening at his firm, he took the trouble to recommend the applicant elsewhere.

The question sometimes arises about whether it is advisable to answer a newspaper advertisement that only provides a box number identification. The reasons for being wary are numerous and may be justifiable. On the other hand, there can be a number of valid reasons for an employer's anonymity. One is the wish to not arouse unrest within the present firm's organization or to declare its business to competing organizations. If possible, however, try to discern something about the situation before selling too much of your own time or before entering into commitments you may regret.

The answer to all of the hypothetical matters we have discussed must be determined by particular circumstances. You may find yourself among the fortunate individuals for whom opportunity always seems to be waiting without much serious effort going into its search.

PROFESSIONALISM

A profession differs from a vocation by requiring education and an ethical standard for operation.

Once you sign an employment contract with a designing firm, you are a member of the team, and your professional loyalties, in so far as you work through the firm, belong there. Never say anything unfavorable about your employer to outsiders. Keep all of the firm's business to yourself. Do not discuss its clients, materials, or methods, except in a sincere and complimentary manner. This is simply good business decorum, and its spirit is written into the code of the American Society of Interior Designers.

Another excellent professional precept of this organization is that you do not speak disparagingly of a competitor, nor should you consciously seek to influence one of your rival's clients in your favor.

Within the organization try to be as helpful as possible. It is an excellent rule not to communicate too freely about business or personal matters. Study the order of precedent carefully and work in accordance with its regulations. A smoothly running machine will be more serviceable to all concerned.

ADVANCEMENT

As a novice, your first position will probably be as an assistant to a professional interior designer. This is true even though, if you apply within three months of graduation, you can be accepted for allied membership in ASID.

The experience as an assistant should lead, as quickly as possible, to complete responsibility for professional undertakings. Because this is true, try to look ahead and learn beyond your regular job duties. Keep abreast of the markets, and, if possible, do some study and travel to learn of new developments in your field.

It is advisable to make connections in social, community, and civic areas. This should come about naturally and be directed by sincere interests.

LEAVING A POSITION

Upon entering a firm, you should be willing to, and expect to, remain with that firm for an adequate period of time to repay it for what seems commensurate with the training you receive. There is really no benefit in being a gadfly and working for one firm after another.

On the other hand, there may come a time when, for the best interests of all concerned, a change should be made. If this decision occurs for reasons of personal integrity, then the business relationship should be dissolved immediately.

When made for any other reason, it is only professional to give adequate advance notice. You should be willing to remain long enough to train your replacement, if necessary.

And certainly you should leave your office and the company's property in the best possible condition.

For whatever reason you leave, say as little about it as possible. Recriminations will only prove self-detrimental, and boasting about a presumably better new job can do no one good. Such statements are always suspect, and it is only a matter of common sense not to indulge in them. We have frequently said that the department of common sense is a pretty good one in which to train. Don't burn your bridges behind you.

EMPLOYMENT PROSPECTS

We shall pause here to say that employment prospects are for several reasons much better than they were in the past. In the first place, the interior design graduate is far better trained than he or she has ever been. Professional educational associations and higher professional requirements have brought this about.

In the second place, the state of the market has changed. There are more large firms now hiring the interior designer. In the third place, the industrial and business world has now organized itself on a more professional basis and can offer professional opportunities to the prepared person.

The public attitude in respect to interior design has changed. It is no longer regarded as a luxury or an extravagant service.

One need not be told that the furnishings business is not conducted as it was only a short time ago. At one end there is the warehouse business which, though it answers a need, scarcely offers the know-how and the merchandise which could be procured from good stores in the past. To a large extent, quality materials and service are most easily obtained through the interior design profession. This is particularly true if a total plan involves a comparatively large variety of materials. However, this in no way means that the profession of interior design acts merely in the function of sales force for industry.

With the right training, your chances for the career in which you have studied are indeed good. The remuneration will depend upon your training, on you, and upon the manner of your commitment. It, too, will probably be good.

CHAPTER 6

CUSTOM DESIGNING

A STUDIO OF YOUR OWN

Custom designing and *private practice* are descriptive terms which are frequently applied to designing for the unique needs of individual clients. Such designing is the opposite of planning for a corporate client who has more standardized requirements. It carries the suggestion of exclusiveness and high cost, both of which are connotations held over from an earlier period of designing for the wealthy. Today the phrase frequently means that the created interiors are planned for the satisfaction of one person or a small number of people and that the client desires a personalized solution.

Specifically we are talking about interior designing by a small studio for the needs of clients who may be furnishing a home or some not-too-large enterprise such as a clubhouse, a small restaurant, a library, or a store. The stamp of one-of-a-kind is present.

The financial structure of such a studio may be organized around private ownership, a partnership, or a small corporation. The greater the number of business participants, the less the individual financial risk but likewise the less possibility of allowing particular taste, standards, and choice of clients.

While private practice may be one of the most rewarding ways of conducting the profession of interior design, it is not the way of the novice. It is better to gain experience under a competent designer before opening up a private studio. The reasoning is understandable—with personal risk-taking the greater can be the individual's financial loss if the owner-designer is not capable both as designer and as business administrator.

In setting up an interior design studio of your own, you will need the services of both business and the law. You will have acquired some knowledge of each in the course of your academic study. It might be wise to supplement this with extracurricular study.

Should you enter the business in partnership with others, remember that the ability to judge people is the basis of much success in this world. Know well your colleagues and their skills and integrity before sharing your career with them.

THE START

Whatever your manner of operating, you need capital (money). How much? In round figures, about enough to run the establishment from four to six months or until the firm has been able to turn over an inventory and operate in the black.

Where does the money come from? Possibly some from your savings or from those of your family, maybe some from the bank or even from supply houses, some from (if you propose a corporation) issued stock.

You will need to establish your credit rating. This should be with a first-rate credit-rating firm which will, for a fee, also assist you in determining your clients' credit ratings. Business runs on credit, so you can understand the importance of this aid.

Your customers and your business should pay promptly—the one guarantees interest, the other discounts. Delay in paying debts, or paying on installments, is costly and must be charged for. Incidentally, the credit-rating firm and your suppliers will prove to be your best friends when you need financial advice. It is to their benefit that you stay in business.

What do you need money or credit for? The first necessity is a place of business. Remember that at least one room used exclusively for this purpose is a professional requisite. The cost of this is charted against business, so that if you use space in your home, you will be remunerated for it on the accounts and with the IRS.

There will be a small sum required to attractively design your quarters. You should keep this expense to the minimum. Use your creative talents and your brawn to make it interesting and expressive of your taste.

You must obtain an initial inventory of samples and furnishing catalogues. There was a day when these were loaned gratuitously. Now they must be purchased. You will thus find it wise to limit your selection, keeping the inventory of the firms with which you will deal to as few as are commensurate with the type of work you propose to do. The present market has central design centers or showrooms in many large cities where it is often possible to take a client to see what you have in mind. Thus you need not keep so large an inventory in your own office.

There are, of course, business expenses—a cost accounting system to be installed, possibly a secretary or accountant to manage business details. Perhaps a computer will simplify this labor.

You must find reliable workroom service. Sometimes such is so in demand that a retaining fee is exacted. This work must pay its own way in addition to paying for your time, skill—and guarantee.

You are entitled to some small wage even at the very early stage of the enterprise. Unfortunately, as owner-business manager, your personal salary is paid last rather than first. The profit on the capital must come first. You may have to exist on your savings for a time.

You must keep some money accessible. It is a rule of thumb that one should have on hand enough capital to pay for installments on large purchases both of goods and equipment.

Capital is wealth no matter how gained. The purpose of business is to put this capital to work so that it will yield financial returns. As the manager of your business, this is your first responsibility.

Keeping your business solvent will require hard work, attention to management, and favorable economic conditions. Your company is not just your personal toy to satisfy your desire to create. It is a hard-won reality in which you keep expenses to the minimum and income to the maximum (regulated by the code of ethics) in order to accomplish your ends.

The business of interior design requires that you obtain a sufficient number of clients to justify your capital expenditure and that you keep them satisfied. This is accomplished by selling a good product: a good design service. This is where your designing skill and your personality enter the picture.

These abilities do not always join in one person. So before you think of a studio of your own, appraise yourself and either take in a partner who can supplement your talents with business acumen or join a firm where you are freed from business worries.

If you decide on custom designing, you will be bringing together people, materials, equipment, and the necessary expertise and will be directing them in such a way as to provide the public with a necessary and worthwhile design service.

IMPORTANCE OF CUSTOM DESIGN

Your work will probably be with individual customers and often concern homes or private offices. As one designer who handled little else for years has said, "I can rest knowing I have helped make numbers of people happy." You have used your skill in outstanding and much-needed service to people, not a bad aim on the chalkboard of life.

Private practice is a very important aspect of interior design and one that is apt to be overlooked in the swing to large enterprise. It may be high time we return to dignifying the individual operation, especially as directed to the residential area.

CHAPTER 7

CONTRACT DESIGNING

Just like the phrase *custom designing,* the term *contract designing* is ambiguous. Generally, it means designing under contract for big business.

There are said to be five factors to business: (1) the product or service to be sold, (2) the seller, (3) the public that wants or needs this product or service, (4) the money, and (5) the manner of management or the efficient connecting of the others. These concepts will help us understand the meaning of contract designing.

A contract is a legal agreement between producer and receiver, and it generally applies whether in written or verbal form. Large businesses make such use of the written contract that the manner of doing business itself is so named. Here it implies that a specific agreement with respect to the nature of the work and the manner of fulfilling the assignment is legally bound in contract form. Firms which deal with the public on these terms are considered to be contract firms.

Contract firms usually handle large jobs costing considerable money. Much of the work involves use of identical specified products, as when a hospital assignment requires many beds. A contract order may likewise require some custom-made, one-of-a-kind articles. An interior designer working with a contract firm will be known as a contract interior designer, one doing business under the contract method.

Contract work is generally highly specialized. A contract firm may use the services of a score of drafters or computer experts (CAD designers). It may employ designers who specialize in planning the interiors of churches, schools, hospitals, retirement homes, and many other types of buildings. It may use space planners; specialists in lighting, color, equipment, plumbing, heating, and possibly safety; certainly specs writers; and schedule managers. All these workers are skilled in some phase of interior designing. Contract designing is a multifaceted process requiring cooperation in order to supply the client's needs.

Contract designing, then, implies working on large projects involving much equipment duplication. It is performed under a specified contract, and usually the designer is a member of a large designing firm.

THE CLIENT AND THE FIRM

And who is the client? Often it is another large corporation—a hospital, hotel, restaurant, office, or merchandising establishment. And don't forget the government as a client. Both designer and client are part of the big industrial-business complex that is the world today. There can scarcely be any other method of handling the design problems of such clients than the method we are now describing. In response to such need, the contract branch of interior designing has emerged today. It has grown by leaps and bounds over the last few decades.

THE SUPPLIERS

The contract branch of interior design in turn is supported by a gigantic army of specialized trades and industries, some of which have their own designers on their staffs. Such affiliations have the disadvantage of limiting the designer's choice of selection. On the other hand, a designer working for a particular industrial firm may have a close understanding related to need and product.

THE FINANCIAL ASPECT OF CONTRACT DESIGNING

Contract designing has come about in answer to a need. It is a phenomenon largely of the last quarter-century, and it is one that shows no sign of abatement. Therefore, there is some justification in speaking of a split in interior design areas between those devoted to the private and generally smaller production and those that engage in large contracts. It must be understood, however, that such a cleavage is largely nominal.

One principal difference may well be in the financial method each predominantly uses. Several systems, however, could be arranged for any undertaking, each especially suited to some portion of the work. The custom designer may be remunerated by a fee, a commission, a percentage of the total order, or a salary. The contract firm, on the other hand, more often operates on a contract basis, receiving a percentage of the total bill. But it, too, may deal on a consultation fee basis for services performed. So long as the terms are clearly set forth and agreed upon by both parties—ethical ones—it does not much matter what method is employed.

If contract work is paid for as percentage of the total commodity bill, the percentage per item is of course much lower than it would have to be in custom work. There is a difference between the amount of time required in specifying 100 duplicate chairs and the amount of time needed to detail 100 separate ones. This difference results in a higher mark-up per individual article in custom assignments.

ADVANTAGES AND DISADVANTAGES FOR THE YOUNG DESIGNER

What is the advantage to the young designer in entering contract work rather than private practice? In the first place, a job may be more available. If the new graduate has some particular skills and feels more suited to specialized work, there may be greater opportunity to use those talents in a contract design firm.

There are likewise disadvantages in contract designing. You are never more than part of a finished product, even though you may have participated in group action from beginning to end. There is not quite the sense of involvement nor the satisfaction of an individually conceived and executed project. Nor is there the same amount of publicity attained from a successful one. You will be first, last, and always a member of the team—practically anonymous. This situation, of course, varies with the size of the firm and with its policy.

Again, contract work is probably more lucrative than an individual practice could be, and it is more enlarging of your range of experience. You learn from observation of large design complexes.

HOW THE WORK PROGRESSES

How does the work progress in a contract office? First, the office must get a client. Out-and-out advertising is generally taboo with most design firms. However, all the successful work done by your firm helps to create an image, to interest and attract customers.

Your client, of course, may be considering other firms. Therefore, there will have to be preliminary meetings to set forth the client's needs. These meetings will be followed by a proposal, suggesting solutions with drawn plans and costs. This proposal may be presented to a committee of people interested in the wants of the purchaser. This is always one of the more difficult encounters, because a committee is one of the most troublesome of aggregate bodies to handle successfully, another important skill to learn.

These preliminaries are as necessary and costly as the size and the expense of the project warrants. This phase of the work is time consuming and, unfortunately, may, in the end, be unrewarding. That is the chance inherent in this sort of endeavor even when some form of compensating indemnity may be in order for unsuccessful schemes.

In such large enterprises, legal advice is necessary along the way. Before signing a final agreement, the firm must have guaranteed itself against inflation, against the financial future of its client, against any chance of the client's wishing to retract at some future time.

Obviously a contract business is one involving much capital. In January 1994, *Interior Design* magazine reported that fees for the top 100 giants were just over $600 million (p. 31). (Figures reported represent the period between July 1, 1992, and June 30, 1993). Such statistics offer a quantity rather than a quality gauge; nevertheless, no firm can long perform on such a scale if its work is unsatisfactory.

Early in the undertaking, if the contract firm is not primarily an architectural one with an interior design department, it may be necessary to establish a professional relationship with the architect who is connected with the project in question. It is important that the architect be informed of the interior design requirements related to architectural, mechanical, electrical, and plumbing systems. Such information must be itemized, costs detailed, and cost liabilities assigned. All participants must know exactly which of the contributing firms will perform certain obligations and from which budget the cost must come. Time schedules require coordination.

In short, a large job cannot be like the orange—peeled in discrete layers; the sinews are interlocked and cling to one another.

As design education is progressing to a better understanding of such interrelated problems, interior designers, architects, and landscapists are generally working well together. In this partnership each of the environmentalists has much to offer, and their coordination may well lead to advantageous developments in the future.

From this point, the work in a contract design firm progresses much as described in earlier chapters. It is a question of scheduling, spec writing, confirmation of orders, business accounting, installations, work supervision, inspections, and final payments, plus frequently some sort of gala affair to celebrate completion.

In many respects contract work is no different from any project in the design field except that it is larger and by implication involves far more repetitive installments. Hence, it is usually financed in a different way, may place you in the role of a more specialized designer, and may possess greater remunerative possibility.

YOU AND THE CONTRACT FIRM

If you have graduated in good standing from an accredited and highly regarded school, you may upon application find yourself accepted in a prestigious contract firm. You will probably serve at first in some minor capacity, wherever your skills are most needed and useful, and you will learn much.

If you prove yourself deserving, you will be placed in the circle where the real designing occurs. Perhaps your title will be that of junior designer.

With some expertise you may be given a job where you are known as the designer in charge of the project. This means that you will have the overall responsibility of seeing that the team's concept is carried out. The designing itself will probably not be entirely your work but rather that of the group. Contract work is company work. However, at this point, your name may appear whenever the project gets publicity. Reputable firms are generous about giving credit because the firm's name appears along with the designer's.

In the course of time, you may become the senior designer. Then you will not only have your name affixed to a design project but also will place your stamp on all projects.

CONTRACT DESIGN AND THE FUTURE

As large projects have grown to need—or at least to request—the service of both interior design and architecture, some method of cooperation and of operation had to be devised to use the talents of each discipline while giving each its just reward. Contract designing will grow as a method of professionally satisfying a public need in our urbanized industrial civilization.

This progression of the designing professions will have to keep abreast of all new technology. This will mean an even greater dependence on the computer. There is coordination of tasks which rely on computer services. Through it the designer will have access to a designing tool; a data recall system; a financial recording system; and engineering process planning, implementation, and coordination of projects every step of the way.

One important innovation has already occurred. It is a result of the needs of contract designing and the capabilities inherent in the computer. Due to the need for accuracy, for easy availability, for large quantities of data, an efficient means of recall is part of today's designing picture.

Thus designing firms are negotiating for future work with clients. The original designing firm keeps all data relative to the original task and thus is in position to set up schedules for renovation or replacement of equipment or of background details. These recall data have their price and could be sold to an establishment by a design firm, Thus, for instance, a hospital could place its renovating on a schedule which could quite easily be determined and its cost ascertained. Another move toward regimentation, another possibility for service, another way to reward.

CHAPTER 8

RELATED FIELDS

OPPORTUNITIES WITHIN THE PROFESSIONAL CAREER

There are many career opportunities open to those who have trained in interior design. It is well to consider them because circumstances may prevent you from following the career for which you are educated.

Also, you may complete the required course of study for professional work and then find that your interests lie along the line of some specialty within this career, such as lighting, color, or space planning. Specializing could likewise be oriented toward specific and current social interests such as energy control, sound control, or safety conditioning. One of these interests might become your specialty to use within a designing firm or in a more extensive arena.

Study or do research in your chosen specialty. Gain some satisfactory achievement, however small, in respect to it; have this publicized and solicit more work in this area.

From there on, keep the ball rolling. Each new job becomes a learning experience, and if successfully carried out, an indirect advertisement. Probably in time your specialty will become your major activity.

OPPORTUNITIES FOR THOSE WITH PROFESSIONAL OR PARAPROFESSIONAL TRAINING

There are many positions which are indirectly related to your interior design training that may appeal to you. They are listed in alphabetical order.

Antiques

Some interior design students are interested in using the historical knowledge they have acquired in the sphere of antiques—dealing in, appraising, writing about, restoration of. These jobs can range up and down the financial ladder.

As has often been said, dealing in antiques is not a business; it is a mania, and those so afflicted need scarcely be told how to obtain a position in the field. But you must know the goods and the class of furnishings with which you desire to deal.

Depending upon your credentials, look for work with some reputable or nationally known dealer. Write to and for this magazine:

Antiques
Bryant Publications, Inc.
575 Broadway
New York, NY 10012

Study the magazine; visit museum collections; train your eye to distinguish between the real and the spurious. Develop your selling ability. Help people make decisions which you think are to their advantage as well as your own.

Commission Art

This is artwork either as your own agent or with an independent firm which sells its services. One such is a group of traveling artists who engage for a fee to illustrate the accomplishments of a designer or design firm.

Obviously this sort of service demands the highest degree of a specialized delineation skill. This is one kind of activity where a picture is worth a thousand words.

Even a unique and glamorous style of rendering may please an advertising firm. A line quality may gain a reputation for you. Exhibit wherever possible and advantageous. You are probably safe from imitation.

Computer Management

We have no doubt said enough about computers. However, under the present discussion it should be added that there is opportunity for one skilled both in computerology and in interior design to sell his or her services to individual firms for the purpose of teaching and coordinating the new computer uses within the designer's field of operation. Here you will have to be on your own. This field is for the skilled, the imaginative, and the enterprising.

Consultant

One type of position offers consulting services for a fee to clients. Even other interior designers occasionally have need for outside advice.

First, you need a good designing reputation. Second, you need at least the basic color charts, samples, probably a photograph library, or access to the showrooms.

On the other hand, you may be surprised that some clients are simply anxious to have someone to talk to about their problem.

However, for the sake of your own conscience, it is wise to have adequate qualification before hanging out your shingle.

Crafts

Here we need not give advice. The craftworker is self-motivated. The skill may have been learned—weaving, woodworking, metal working, ceramics, even painting—in the interior design courses which have been taken. Nothing will prevent the true artisan from performing with expertise.

However, of course, a craftworker's abilities will need testing in local exhibits.

Designer with Building Development Firms

Some designing positions do not demand, although they may use, professional interior design service. For example, a firm that builds development housing frequently needs a designer to set up model suites in new areas. Such a position frequently offers the allure of travel, as a large firm frequently builds both nationally and internationally.

The chance to design such models may not be readily available. However, begin to check with your local contracting companies. One clue often leads to another. It is not a bad idea to obtain an office assignment in any firm which does this sort of business. Learn about that firm and the caliber of its work. When satisfied, then begin to suggest your abilities.

Display and Exhibition Positions

This kind of work calls upon talents similar to those used in stage designing, although historical accuracy is not so frequently necessary. Creating displays for stores is only one aspect of such work. Display artists are likewise employed by industrial companies for traveling exhibitions. There is need for personnel to arrange changing presentations for the merchandise marts and showrooms. Even museums use designers for planning the backgrounds for their exhibitions.

Learn who heads the display work at your local stores. One can sometimes help with a community group that wants to put forward its image. After all, displays are forms of advertising. If you have the inclination, cultivate the talent.

Equipment Specialist

Frequently such firms as those that deal in kitchen supplies or other furnishing equipment will have a specialist on their staff to show the positioning of their equipment to a customer. Additional training with specific equipment will be an aid. Often home economics courses will help. Then apply at local or district offices specializing in such equipment.

Fashion Forecaster

This is one way of giving direction to the market or forecasting fashion trends to the public. One who gains a good historical background in interior design acquires a certain sense about how to forecast the future from interpreting the culture of the past.

Try your hand at writing some articles for the local paper or for one of the better magazines. Nothing, you know, succeeds like success.

Government Work

The question about designing for the government has often been asked. The White House has occasionally had its bursts of designer-effected renovation which reflected the aesthetics of the age (for example, the Tiffany restoration of the early 1900s), but government offices and buildings—even our embassies—received no systematic attention.

There is a Federal Design Improvement program of the U. S. government and a Foreign Buildings Operations of the Department of State. However, much of the design work is contracted by private industry.

Historic Preservation and Restoration

This large and upcoming calling may provide specialized work for both professional and paraprofessional interior designers. It is an area which has come prominently before the public during the last quarter-century due to the laudable activities of the National Trust for Historic Preservation.

The address of the trust is:

National Trust for Historic Preservation
1785 Massachusetts Avenue NW
Washington, DC 20036

The trust is not a government agency; it is primarily an advisory and educational organization devoted to the preservation of the nation's landmarks.

Historic preservation uses the expertise of the interior designer who has specialized in the history of buildings and furnishings. This knowledge extends to restoration procedures. Above all, it must not be superficial.

Adaptive reuse is an important phase of this work. In this phase, old buildings are adapted to today's purposes while still preserving the spirit of their own age. The question any designer will have to ask is whether he or she is wise enough to interpret the spirit of the past. When you can answer in the affirmative, your study of history has arrived at the point of maturity.

The positions which may be available will range all up and down the economic ladder, and you may have to ferret them out. There is writing and television communicating to be done. There are some positions with local agencies that are engaged in actual restoration. There is work with historical libraries.

Get involved in what a local group interested in historic buildings is doing. Of course show your interest in every way you can—speeches, articles, renderings, participation in local trips.

Check with your city government. Is it proposing to do something in the nature of historic preservation with respect to some area of the city? Can you speak to civic groups about this? Can you approach architectural firms to see if they have any such commitments?

If one is interested in this field, one should choose a preparatory school carefully. Some colleges, for instance, specialize in historic orientation, particularly in their graduate studies.

Museum Work

Much work in museums is concerned with the decorative arts. There are entry-level positions on the lecturing, restoration, curatorial, and teaching staffs. The best advice is to apply at a local museum and keep learning. It is one of the great advantages of this kind of work that you do gain knowledge from your associations.

Photography

Some people find the photographing of interiors a specialty that is even more challenging than interior design itself. However, it involves knowledge of both professions. Can you photograph so as to convey the sense of the space organization, convey the emotional tone, focus the objects on the viewer's attention? It is a real skill and art, and one often involving considerable expenditure for equipment.

Photograph your own or a colleague's designs and try to have the results published in a local magazine or paper. A lead photograph of an interior by some prominent designer might be done in a way sufficiently outstanding to gain some recognition.

Just keep plugging away, and watch your opportunity. There is no field where expertise rather than partial attainment should be more rewarded.

Stage Designing

We shall say little about this except that your training as an interior designer is admirably suited for this type of work. Most plays need stage sets, and you can make them effective, authentic in style, and perhaps improvise them at the lowest cost. Try for volunteer work at your local community theater. You may have to give much in time, labor, and skill in order to receive any reward. Nevertheless, it will pay off. Genius will win out.

Store-Home Consultant

Advisory positions which do not require the expertise of a professional interior designer are frequently available in the furnishings department of large stores. Usually such employment ties in closely with the merchandise of a particular store. The sort of position we are describing is frequently found in stores that do not feature an interior design department.

Teaching

As we have been arranging our notations alphabetically, the career of teaching happens to come near the last on the list. That is patently not true with respect to its worth. While possibly not ranking tops in remuneration—although today salaries are not disreputable—it has done a great deal in behalf of placing interior design on the list of professions.

On the subject of salaries, one must consider the fact that most teaching contracts are for a school year of nine months. They often include confirmation of a sabbatical year for study and a tenure track for the possibility of promotion and guarantee of permanency of position.

Credentials must be at least a master's degree for teaching at college level, and a Ph.D. is preferred. There is considerable discussion concerning the need for experience in the profession. While this is quite understandable (as in a medical internship), it would seem that it should not be a substitute but rather an addition to sound academic training. Inasmuch as guided field work is often included throughout the course of study, experience will come with a diploma.

Today if you wish to teach interior design, positions are available. There is scarcely a week when we do not receive a notice from some qualified source that is seeking a teacher of interior design. Usually these requests are for specialized areas of expertise, such as design, rendering, workroom practices, or business disciplines.

Fringe benefits are good. The pensions in state universities are adequate and sure. It is not an ivory tower sinecure, however. The teacher is expected to integrate with the professional organization and with the community educational activities. This probably means some travel and speaking engagements in the surrounding areas, some participation in community educational affairs, and certainly membership in IDEC, with attendance at its meetings and possibly the acceptance of a role in its work. You will be expected to do writing in professional journals.

Your reward? For those of you who enjoy study, who care to organize and impart your thoughts about such a challenging subject—from the aesthetic, the philosophic, the utilitarian, or the historic point of view—there could be no better calling. We would totally deny George Bernard

Shaw's dictum that "those who can, do, and those who can't, teach."

Application can be made through IDEC. However there is no need; if you have the will and the credentials, the job will hunt you.

Television

The tube has fill-in positions for those who can report on fashion in apparel and in interior furnishings. If one is wishing to report on the latter exclusively, possibly a reputation will have to be first earned. It is hoped—but not assured—that such reportage would be of the highest order.

You should first know your subject and be able to project enthusiasm for it to others. You should have a good grounding, especially in aesthetics and history. This may not be called to the fore but its absence shows up disastrously. What a challenge!

We all know that probably the chief requisite is to be beautiful or handsome and to possess glamour and have a pleasant speaking voice. While in school take some drama and voice culture courses.

Writing

In this work, merit will gain its reward. For some, this may come early in life; for others, only after years of effort. It is like several other careers suggested in this listing: those who like to write, who enjoy marshaling words to express their thoughts, and who feel that there is much to be said about the subject matter we have been talking about will naturally gravitate toward using the printed word. Caution: don't expect to get rich—remuneration is unpredictable.

First select your audience and then your type of vehicle—newspaper, fashion magazine, book. Take courses in English and in literature. One who would write must speak well and like to read good writing. There is no area in interior design where the need is greater.

Certainly we have not listed all possible opportunities. To do so would be almost repetitious and certainly boring. The training in interior design today, by the very fact that the profession touches on so many aspects of life, has to be extensive. A little imagination, and it can constitute an entry wedge into many different kinds of opportunities. A bit of initiative, and you won't lack for employment.

Have the desire, get the training, and seek your niche.

CHAPTER 9

PROFESSIONAL ORGANIZATIONS

DEFINING A PROFESSION

The final definition of *profession* has never been precisely determined. It is enough to use the meaning given in Chapter 2, the meaning sanctioned by dictionary and encyclopedia. A profession is a calling requiring specialized education and adherence to a code of ethics. It is customary to suggest the existence of a supportive professional organization whose members fulfill and uphold prescribed requirements. A profession gains recognition in the law through government licensing.

Although attempted throughout history, professionalism thus rigidly ordered has been a relatively late arrival on the social and legal scene. In the 1600s, for instance, the surgeon as well as the physician might have been merely the apothecary.

WHY PROFESSIONAL ORGANIZATIONS EXIST

A professional organization is a group of professional people who have banded together primarily because they have mutual occupational interests.

Such an organization has four major purposes: to improve its collective image, to help the young establish a continuity in the profession, to create mutually helpful relations with similar organizations, and to contribute toward social good. Such an organization must uphold an educational standard and must subscribe to a code of ethics in order to obtain professional goals. The following professional organizations serve these purposes for the field of interior design.

THE AMERICAN INSTITUTE OF INTERIOR DESIGN (AIID)

The earliest American organization within the group then known as interior decorators took place in 1931. At that time, a need was felt for the services of practitioners who would have a broader concept of their purpose and who would represent a more extensive geographical territory than the few local organizations then existing.

It is of interest and importance that this first consolidation on a national scale was prompted by the Great Depression of 1929. The high-standard furniture industry of Grand Rapids, Michigan, was in imminent danger of financial ruin simply because America did not have enough wealth at that critical time to buy furniture. Wisely, the manufacturers and civic leaders promoted a consolidation of American decorators for the purpose of dealing more effectively with the mutually shared financial crisis.

THE AMERICAN SOCIETY OF INTERIOR DESIGNERS (ASID)

Following several changes of name and organizational adjustments—in 1936 the AIID was changed to American Institute of Decorators (AID)— in 1975 the present American Society of Interior Designers (ASID) was founded. It was in that year that the AID joined with another existing association, the National Society of Interior Designers (NSID). The purpose of the union is clear; it was to strengthen each organization through a merger.

This consolidated group of professional interior designers is the largest organization of its kind in the world. Its membership is now 18,000. ASID is not the only interior design organization, but it is the oldest and largest. Check trade publications and yellow page listings for the names of other interior design professional organizations.

The ASID is open to all qualified designers regardless of their special field—private practice, contract, institutional, or government work. The organization is thus the one effective body able to advance the needs of all who are professionally practicing under its jurisdiction. The professional members of the organization may place the initials "ASID" after their names.

Within the total membership, there are divisional groups which function in a somewhat similar manner to that of the individual states of the United States. At present the ASID has 49 divisional chapters and one international chapter.

ASID Group Responsibilities

The first of the group responsibilities of ASID is education. ASID sets the educational requirements for its membership, and it assists the educational facilities of the nation in maintaining high and relevant standards for the education of interior designers.

In addition to working on all phases of educational improvement, ASID mandates that its members and the schools which carry out its educational purposes be equipped with the latest knowledge of theory or fact bearing on the profession. This means keeping abreast of information on many topics, such as new materials, technology, building codes, government regulations, flammability standards, design psychology, and product performance. This educational progress is accomplished through sponsored academic courses, seminars, group meetings, workshops, and a program of self-teaching exercises (STEP). Thus, the interior design profession keeps up-to-date.

The second of the professional functions of the ASID has been the establishment of a code of ethics under which it operates.

Members of the American Society of Interior Designers are required to conduct their professional practice in a manner that will command the respect and confidence of their clients, suppliers, colleagues, and the general public. Every member of the society subscribes to a professional code which upholds the laws and regulations of the group regarding business procedures and the practice of interior design. It states clearly the allowable manner of functioning with respect to compensation, competence in execution, and details of written contract.

A member must proceed in accordance with the highest professional standards. He or she is pledged to secrecy with regard to privileged information from a client. The code further outlines the professional allegiance of the members to the society itself and to allied professions.

Kinds of ASID Memberships

Several kinds of membership are included in ASID. Professional membership guarantees that the member has the educational and ethical qualifications to practice interior design.

Another kind of membership is student membership. Student chapters are located in schools offering training in interior design. These organizations are intended to create desirable professional ties to ASID during the student years. Speakers from the professional organization are frequently featured. ASID conducts field trips for the benefit of students. Competitions and grants, scholarships, and awards also are part of the student program. Presently there are 215 student chapters of ASID.

Students who apply within 90 days of their graduation are automatically accorded allied membership in ASID. Allied membership includes practitioners who have not yet completed their examination requirements. They are at present known as Allied Member ASID.

The allied membership likewise includes those who are engaged in the educational phases of interior design; those who are primarily involved in professional activities allied to the profession of interior design such as architecture, historic restoration, and museum work; and those who are actively involved in some form of press reporting.

The ASID program reaches out into the community through exhibitions, symposiums, restorations, and press articles. It is an active organization within the accountability to its interests.

The work of ASID benefits its members, schools, and the public in incalculable ways and has involved many hours and much unselfish labor on the part of its members. The organization has constantly striven to create its true image in society. It is hoped that all who enter the field in the future will be mindful of this great debt which they owe to the past years of the society and will continue to uphold its purposes.

The address of the society's national headquarters is:

The American Society of Interior Designers
608 Massachusetts Avenue N.E.
Washington, DC 20002

The ASID publishes numerous folders describing its work. These are available from headquarters.

INTERIOR DESIGN EDUCATORS COUNCIL (IDEC)

In 1963 a group of education associates of the ASID (then called AID) formed the Interior Design Educators Council (IDEC) for the purpose of studying various aspects of the education of future interior designers. IDEC was incorporated in 1968. Since its inception, IDEC has grown both in numbers and accomplishments.

Active membership in IDEC is open to people who are engaged in interior design education at levels above high school in schools that feature at least a two-year major course of study in interior design. These schools must meet the same academic requirements as other schools of comparable levels.

IDEC biannually publishes the *Journal of Interior Design Education and Research (JIDER),* an excellent agent for reporting educational and research material in the field. This journal is just one of the scholastic activities of the Interior Design Educators Council.

The mailing address of IDEC is:

Interior Design Educators Council
14252 Culver Drive, Suite A331
Irving, CA 92714

IDEC has pamphlets available describing its work.

FOUNDATION OF INTERIOR DESIGN EDUCATION RESEARCH (FIDER)

IDEC has been most successful in its chosen tasks. Among its achievements are several enterprises which are now supervised by special organizations whose membership is composed of chosen delegates from several professional undertakings concerned with interior design. One of the most important of these is FIDER, the Foundation for Interior Design Education Research. This organization is charged with the accrediting of schools of interior design.

The prime responsibility for accreditation of professional programs in the United States resides with the National Committee on Accreditation and with the U.S. Office of Higher Education through its Accreditation and Institutional Eligibility Advisory Committee. These bodies then delegate special responsibilities in individual professions to specific and designated groups representing the professions or fields concerned.

Through these channels FIDER is charged with the accreditation of schools and programs of interior design.

The basis of this accreditation is subdivided into:

- Program objectives
- Educational program
- Students
- Faculty
- Resources and facilities
- Administration
- Relations to outside community

FIDER publishes *A Guide to the FIDER-Accredited Interior Design Programs in North America.* It can be obtained from FIDER for $17.50 a copy. It also publishes a directory of interior design programs accredited by FIDER. This is free of charge and can be obtained by writing FIDER.

The official address for FIDER is:
60 Monroe Center N.W.
Grand Rapids, MI 49503-2920

INTERNATIONAL FEDERATION OF INTERIOR DESIGNERS (IFI)

Although ASID represents the largest professional organization of interior designers in the United States, there are strong organizations in the international field, especially in Canada and Europe. These have banded together under the title of the International Federation of Interior Designers (IFI). This organization is, as its name implies, a federation. Many separate countries also have their own associations.

INDUSTRY FOUNDATION OF ASID

The Industry Foundation of ASID is composed of firms engaged in supplying equipment, products, or services to the interior design profession. The Industry Foundation thus provides a basis for interaction between the interior design profession and the various industries and crafts which serve it. It is dedicated to advancing research studies concerned with industry and interior design.

For example, when design contests are sponsored by industry, it is desirable that they be studied and approved by the professional sector of an appropriate committee. It is equally important that where the interior design profession has manifested a need for certain kinds of products and equipment, the industry will cooperate in seeing that the problem is studied and a solution made. The Industry Foundation operates under the auspices of ASID.

NATIONAL COUNCIL FOR INTERIOR DESIGN QUALIFICATION (NCIDQ)

This council supervises the qualifying examination for interior design professional competence. This two-day examination, part written and part pictorial, is required of people who wish to qualify as competent for professional interior designer status. It contains interior design theory and practical testing for interior designing. A professional member of ASID must pass the NCIDQ examination.

The address for NCIDQ is:

National Council for Interior Design Qualification
50 Main Street
White Plains, NY 10606-1920

INTERIOR DESIGNERS OF CANADA (IDC)

The Interior Designers of Canada is an organization similar to ASID. It is an associate member of IFI.

The address for IDC is:

Interior Designers of Canada
Ontario Design Center, Suite 414
260 King Street, East
Toronto, Ontario
Canada M5A IK3

LICENSING

When a professional group grows sufficiently large and proficient, when its course of requisite study becomes recognized and formalized, and when practicing in the involved career without the proper training would be deemed harmful to the people of a state (on the bases of health, safety, welfare), then the state can make it unlawful to follow that career without first obtaining legal permission. This legalizing process is generally known as licensing of the profession. Sections of the procedure are often designated as Practice Act and Name Entitlement.

In the pursuit of licensing it is particularly important that interior designers be knowledgeable about governmental codes, standards, and regulations that protect public health and safety.

The interior design profession has now attained some form of licensing in 17 states and in the District of Columbia. Most of the other states are progressing toward this goal.

Licensing usually entails the passing of a state examination for competency in the profession as well as entitlement through the comprehensive professional examination (NCIDQ). Adherence to a code of ethics, which is basic to a professional organization, is of course upheld.

The ASID Code of Ethics states: "The designer shall conform to existing laws, regulations and codes governing business procedures and the practice of interior design as established by the state or community in which he or she practices."

CHAPTER 10

INTERNATIONAL INTERIOR DESIGN

SIMILARITIES AND DIFFERENCES

An assemblage of five ordinary wicker armchairs that had been produced in five different countries provided a fascinating revelation. The basic designs and purposes of the chairs were similar. All were attractive and functional. One chair was made in Italy, another in Germany, one in Scandinavia, another in the United States, and one in Japan. When seeing the chairs side by side, any sensitive viewer should have been able to attach the right source to each. The international market and the international organizations in interior design which use it in their work present the intriguing picture of subtle national differences within essentially similar frameworks.

Any discussion of international interior design separates into three distinct parts: the organization of the profession in each country, the influence of the American profession abroad, and the educational exchange of students and faculty.

PROFESSIONAL ORGANIZATION

International interior design has its professional organization, the International Federation of Interior Designers (IFI).

As the name implies, it is a federation of the organizations of the individual participating countries. Strongly represented are Austria, Belgium, Canada, Denmark, Finland, France, Germany, Great Britain, Holland, Hungary, Iceland, Italy, Norway, Poland, Sweden, Switzerland, and the United States.

The IFI has a professional code which in essence is similar to that of ASID. It deals with both the aesthetic and the ethical practices prescribed by the profession. In the latter, particularly with respect to the mode of business practices, the IFI is probably more precise than the ASID.

The reason for any such difference may derive from the fact that interior design work in the United States has been forced to face the question of designing for the business world and thus of effecting some solution to contract designing. The European code rests more on proscriptions; the American seems to suggest a professional partnership among designer, business, and client.

The IFI holds biannual international congresses to which an American delegate of both ASID and IDEC attend as nonvoting members. Important congresses have been held in Vienna, Paris, Helsinki, and the United States.

The general level of design expertise illustrated at these assemblies is said to be of high quality. In the education curriculum as prescribed abroad, more emphasis is placed on cabinetry and detailing than is found in the United States. Indeed, this emphasis on construction holds true for all the artifacts usual to interior furnishings. This experience with the actual fabricating of things leads to a clearer understanding of how they are put together and ultimately to a greater appreciation.

This does not mean that the foreign market deals solely in handmade articles. Manufacture is a strong economic force abroad, although the two types of accomplishment may frequently run separate and parallel.

The address of IFI is:

The International Federation of Interior Designers
P.O. Box 19126
1000 GC Amsterdam
The Netherlands

AMERICAN INTERIOR DESIGN IDEAS ABROAD

Foreign countries react to American ideas. The American influence is seen in motel chains with tastefully and functionally designed rooms. Shopping malls are being built with emphasis on coordinated interior design, on considering space planning so as to route traffic, and on a certain dramatic fun quality that makes shopping a form of entertainment. Hotels are adopting syndicated suavity. These are among the ideas from America that travel and make American interior design profitable in foreign lands.

It is interesting, however, to note that even with American designing, the flavor of the work often resembles that of the host country. Sometimes this native decor is painfully artificial. One then is tempted to think that it, too, is an American import.

This entering of the foreign market by American enterprise is a give-and-take proposition, with each country having something to contribute. It should not be forgotten that some of the finest furnishings, both in quality and in design, come from abroad.

FORMAL EDUCATION EXCHANGE

Formal education exchange between countries involves faculty exchange and visits, cultural exchange of course content, and student-exchange.

A recent concern of both American and foreign interior designers is the exchange of instruction in schools. The implementation of this idea is under the jurisdiction of the cooperative extension service of the professional societies.

Faculty exchange, although it confers many benefits, is an idea that at present has not been implemented on any large scale. Language, financial, and social difficulties are often insurmountable.

However, school curricula in the United States are introducing studies that involve interchange of ideas between students of different cultures. These frequently call for short visits from foreign instructors. Such studies have many advantages. As they are often focused on design in countries which have sent many refugees here—countries of Africa, Southeast Asia, and Latin America—these studies offer opportunity for extensive research, which inevitably leads to better cultural understanding.

And last, but not least, there is the story of student exchange, whether on a short-term basis (as when a school takes a group abroad for a summer session) or for a year of the academic career. Obviously the benefits must include the long-term advantage of language learning, international friendship, and (hopefully) cooperation. Besides, such foreign residence is fun and part of the global experience of the coming age.

CHAPTER 11

THE FUTURE OF INTERIOR DESIGN

A BRIGHT FUTURE

From the standpoint of promising a good position to a qualified person, interior design now has a bright future. In some ways it is a more difficult future to prepare for, it is a future possessing different quality and emphasis from the past.

What is this "someday" for which interior design must prepare? Much of it is already on the docket. It differs from the past in the same manner that one age differs from another. The last half of the twentieth century, in which we are presently living, is characterized by large-scale enterprises, unbelievable standardization encompassing new technologies, and a vast new market. Interior design has made giant strides toward professional service in its dealings with all of this change.

In the process of this growth and alteration, interior design may be in danger of losing its aesthetic approach, replacing it with a functional one. By definition interior design must preserve both.

Let us discuss this new interior design world as it appears today and attempt to predict its future.

LARGE ENTERPRISES

It is scarcely news that the business world is marked by consolidations and mergers or that vast new enterprises are requiring gargantuan headquarters that are designed to impress the world with their magnificence and power as well as their efficiency. This assures much new building or, at very least, renovating and furnishing.

The interior design profession has been affected by such development. This shows first in its own business organizations, which must be large in order to cope. Interior design groups have specialists in every phase of the work.

Many large companies, organized to handle the entire task of building and furnishing, have architects, landscape architects, interior designers, and craftworkers among their members. Sometimes such an assembly is organized under the heading of architecture, sometimes of interior design. It operates as a business concern with the professional groups working independently, much as a number of doctors may operate in a clinic, calling on one another as needed.

In whatever ways it is organized, this large-scale designing company represents an opportunity for an assured position and assured clients who are usually spending such substantial amounts of money that the work is entirely on a contract basis. This sort of operational setup is frequently known as the contract method of operating, and the firm is a contract design firm.

Another aspect of large enterprises, whatever their purpose, is the aspect inherent in business itself. We read much about graft in business, but we tend to forget that the philosophy "let the buyer beware" has largely disappeared from the reputable business world. It has been superceded in most large businesses with the proposition that good business subscribes to ethical structure if it wishes to thrive. The result is that business itself has become more professional in its philosophy.

This development has enabled modes of ethical operation to exist in all phases of the design industry that are dependent on business. Ethics, like sports, breaks down when any player hits below the belt.

STANDARDIZATION OF PRODUCTS

This element of our civilization requires little explanation because it is so prevalent. For instance, it is quite possible for a knowledgeable observer to easily recognize the source of the furniture in a building: this is a Mies van der Rohe chair, that is such-and-such a table. Then when it comes to outfitting the place with computerized equipment, once a model is chosen, the result is impossible to obtain in anything but duplication. This again makes the ordering and installation of the material a contract job, although the initial choice and placement may have been the designer's.

NEW SCIENCE AND TECHNOLOGY

Much new science and technology is already here but never lasts for long. This is an age of discovery and innovation. Much equipment is outmoded almost before it is installed. The designer has a difficult time trying to foresee the future in order to save money for the client.

The most astonishing revolution has been in electronic development. Computerization is here to stay. The interior designer will meet it not only as a field to design for but likewise as a technique that must be mastered during training. It will play a strong role in analysis of client needs, in project coordination, and information retrieval. It is being used by large companies to detail their products, thus doing away with the need for cumbersome and expensive catalogues.

Probably the most fabulous use of computerization is in the design field itself; it is abbreviated to CAD, for computer aided design. Special systems of software have enabled the designing industry to practically eliminate drafting as well as some rendering. Wherever a line or surface can be reduced to many particles, as in photography or printing, the computer can perform the task. To a certain extent, the subtlety of free line drawing and graded color will be lost. However, precision and speed, coupled with the advantage of being able to erase and remedy mistakes, will be gained.

Another plus will be found in the use of computer-activated films in the classroom to teach fundamental space concepts. When students can see changes before their very eyes, the difficult visualization of relationships will be demonstrated in a way that practically no other means can accomplish.

The computer and its specialized program facilities are here to stay. Most students will have the opportunity to gain understanding and mastery of basic computer techniques before they leave high school. This mastery is most desirable.

Certainly the interior design curricula of today will include instruction in all applicable phases of computer technology. If some personalized qualities seem lost by all this mechanization, something that will serve in the much-enlarged scene of the future in interior design will be gained. The computer offers efficiency in use of time, versatility in use of basic installation property, and control of output and records.

Not only do the electronic technologies throw down the gauntlet to the learner, they challenge his or her designing skill. Clients today are likely to ask for a Georgian drawing room or even an office in that style as well as a space for the computer, an electric kitchen, a telephone equipment console, or media room.

A DIFFERENT MARKET

Not only is the modern market of different character, it is of great physical extent. It is not idle prate to say that the market with which some of the large design firms deal is global. American firms have markets and offices in Europe, the Mideast, the Far East, and South America. Foreign countries also have outlets here. This intercommunication opens opportunities for young designers. What are your language skills?

Interior design has not only extended the territory over which it operates, it likewise has extended the field with respect to types of clients. Whereas it began first as a royal prerogative and then became a concern only of the "carriage trade," it now ranges up and down the ladder—government, libraries, schools, hospitals, low-cost housing, and expensive hotels. Such mobility makes the profession one whose future seems quite reasonably assured.

THE CHALLENGE

The challenge of the future develops from today, but it need not emerge from the shortcomings of our present culture. If interior design is really to lead, it must do so as only real and excellent art can do. This means that interior design must:

- regain the quality of good art, wholeness with appeal
- gain a concept of oneness of environmental arts
- implement the aforementioned points at the educational stage

As a means of creating the future along the lines suggested, we make a bold proposal: future interior designers should develop the talent for writing and illustration. We need good critical writing, creative writing divorced from financial bondage, and challenging writing reminiscent of the feisty confessional writing of Frank Lloyd Wright and the lyrical writing of Louis Sullivan. Good writing, far too long neglected, is the challenge of the future.

Interior design as a professional career has come a long way, yet it has further to go. But it has the capabilities.

A FINAL WORD

In the last century there was a tactical formation in the infantry known as the "square." The theory behind its shape was that it afforded protection against attack on any of four sides and that its officers, who were placed in its center rather than at the front as in a line formation, were better able to deflect the thrust if it should unexpectedly come from flank or rear. It was a nice idea—especially for the officers.

Unfortunately, it did not always work. The enemy learned to drive a cavalry wedge into the center from the weakest flank, which threw the formation into such confusion and collapse that no directions could be given and chaotic flight resulted.

In a sense the analogy to interior design can easily be made. Interior design has four aspects—art, science with technology, profession, and business. The leaders are in a position to call upon any front for an advance.

But interior design is not organized for hostile attack. Its intent is to serve. Its organization is rather that of a highly integrated circle or wheel that sends out power from its hub. And at its center will be you, the leaders of tomorrow.

You must be a special kind of person to drive successfully. You have in hand the power to aid people, people with their neverending variety, with their present and future desires. This requires much knowledge and great sensitivity.

We are not speaking facetiously when we say that interior design can be—though it seldom is—a great art, highly complex, and worthwhile. In the last analysis, interior design rests on sensuous material, but it probes the physical and the spiritual.

Art is only as great as the artist. Artists must lead from a position of such deep appreciation of the past and present as to foresee the future. Art is the cutting edge of the times. Don't settle for slick art rather than great art. Don't buy "plenty of nuttin'."

In closing—interior design is not an easy career. Indeed, if well done it is perhaps one of the most difficult, as its worth is finally being understood. As its educational and administrative support are being properly formed, we predict for it a long and worthwhile future.

Is the analogy of interior design with a sphere, with an atom, too far fetched? No.